"This handbook will greatly bless and nurture the small group ministry in your church."

Dr. David Yonggi Cho

SMALL GROUP LEADERS HANDBOOK

". . . and they devoted themselves to the apostles' doctrine and fellowship."

Acts 22:42

WORKING TOGETHER TO BUILD COMMUNITIES
AND TO REACH PEOPLE

FRANK DAMAZIO
&
MARC ESTES

SMALL GROUP LEADERS HANDBOOK

WORKING TOGETHER TO BUILD COMMUNITIES

AND TO REACH PEOPLE

FRANK DAMAZIO
&
MARC ESTES

Published by City Christian Publishing
9200 NE Fremont • Portland, Oregon 97220

Printed in USA

City Christian Publishing is a ministry of City Bible Church, and is dedicated to serving the local church and its leaders through the production and distribution of quality materials. It is our prayer that these materials, proven in the context of the local church, will equip leaders in exalting the Lord and extending His kingdom.

For a free catalog of additional resources from City Christian Publishing, please call 1-800-777-6057 or visit our web site at *www.CityChristianPublishing.com.*

Small Group Leaders Handbook

ISBN: 1-886849-54-4

FOREWORD

My intention as the senior pastor of City Bible Church is to continue building an enduring church with a strong leadership team that sees equipping and releasing lay leaders as their primary ministry. An enduring church must have solid foundational principles which leaders and people can easily discern, learn, own and build upon. As the church grows spiritually and numerically, changes will take place. My specific responsibility as the senior pastor is to process these changes, pace the changes and prepare the leadership and the congregation for the changes.

The essence of a great church is its commitment to change while honoring its core values. Seeing the biblical need for a pastoral structure that pastors each person intentionally is the first step to establishing a broad-base pastoral system with small groups. It is a biblical idea, a practical idea and it works! We have diligently worked to cast congregational vision for the cell group structure and function. We continually are training leaders, month after month, year after year. The key to success of a small group ministry is twofold: the senior pastor's conviction to build this into a core vision, and the leadership team's involvement as small group leaders and/or teachers of small group leaders.

Frank Damazio, Senior Pastor
City Bible Church

INTRODUCTION

Over the past few years we have devoted a great deal of time, energy and finances to the development of small group ministry in our local church. What we have learned has been through the ongoing process of transforming inspirational thoughts into successful, proven methods. The goal and challenge has been to define a biblically-relevant small group ministry philosophy and then to successfully implement these principles into the context of a local church. The result of this process has given us some proven, reproducible principles that have helped in building our church. Our desire is to now serve other local churches by providing you with these proven concepts.

As you begin your small group journey, you must first recognize that there are many successful small group models used in churches today. What makes any model successful is not just its methodologies and organizational structure but more importantly, the foundational principles upon which that model was built.

Regardless of what model you may choose for your local church, it is important that your model is built on biblical principles. Although every church is uniquely different in its vision, values, purpose, philosophies and methodologies, its biblical foundation should be the same. It is from this foundation that all other components are established and uniquely shaped, including small group ministry.

We have taken these principles and communicated them in a practical and relevant manner so that they can be effectively implemented into any local church regardless of its model or methods. In addition, we have also added a great deal of practical suggestions that will assist you in equipping small group leaders. Our prayer is that these materials might assist you in building a vibrant, healthy local church which, in turn, reaches multitudes for the Kingdom.

Equipping the Saints,

Pastor Marc Estes
Director of Pastoral Ministries
City Bible Church

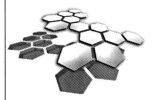

WAYS TO USE THIS HANDBOOK

This handbook has been designed to be used in a variety of formats as listed below. It can be used to systematically teach and equip small group leaders within your church, or used simply as a reference guide to extract pertinent information as needed.

You will find the information organized topically and easy to locate. Each section is broken down into main headings, which are listed in the table of contents. This will allow you to quickly identify the main points of each section and turn to the appropriate area as needed for further review. There are three main ways to use this book:

1. **To Train Small Group Leaders**

   A pastor or designated leader can use this handbook to train and release small group leaders in their church on a regular basis. Furthermore, small group leaders can also use this handbook to train potential leaders within their small group as well. We recommend that those receiving the training have their own *Small Group Leaders Handbook*. Additional copies can be ordered online at *www.CityChristianPublishing.com* or by calling 800-777-6057.

2. **Ongoing Resource Guide**

   This handbook can be used for specific training in any of the areas listed in the table of contents, for district meetings, small group leaders meetings, or church-wide meetings.

   In addition, the handbook can be used as an ongoing resource and referral tool for all small group leaders to review certain principles, ideas, or practical tips as needed.

3. **Personal Study**

   This handbook can be used for personal study or for small group research. If you choose to use it in this format, we recommend that you read it like a book and take the time to apply principles to your own life and ministry. You may also consider taking the time to look up all scriptural references.

This handbook is *not* designed to answer all the questions that may arise while birthing a small group ministry in a local church. Although there are many biblical principles and proven methods that will greatly assist you in this area of planning and development, an entire book would need to be devoted to this one subject alone. If we could serve you in any way regarding the beginning planning and implementation of small group ministry in your local church, please feel free to call City Bible Church at 503-255-2224.

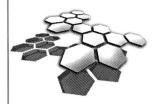

Fill-In Sections: Many sections have places to fill in answers that are given during a teaching time or individual study time. These answers can be found at the back of the handbook on page 149.

Custom Tailoring Handbook to Meet Your Individual Church Needs: There are also sections that allow you to insert your own information that may be specific to your church (e.g. vision of church, structure of church, etc.). When teaching these sections you will want to have information prepared to communicate to the participants that can be inserted during those specific teaching times.

Examples of these fill-in areas, as used at City Bible Church, can be found in the addendum section at the end of this handbook.

Contents

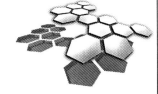

THE VISION OF A NEW TESTAMENT CHURCH

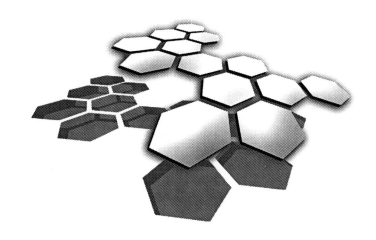

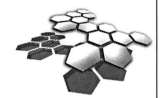

The Vision of a New Testament Church
Chapter One

Defining Vision

From the beginning of time, vision has been the compass that has guided the steps of the human race. Wherever there has been progress, you will find the evidence of vision momentum. We were created by God to receive and implement vision. It is His instrument of advancement.

"A vision without a task is but a dream;
A task without a vision is drudgery;
A vision and a task is the hope of the world."
— Author Unknown

"A blind man's world is bounded by the limits of his touch; an ignorant man's world by the limits of his knowledge; a great man's world by the limits of his vision."
— Paul Hovey

"Give us a clear vision that we may know where to stand and what to stand for, because unless we stand for something, we shall fall for anything."
— Peter Marshall

The Bible makes it clear that we are in absolute need of vision. Vision gives us direction for our future, gives us guidance in our decisions, gives us motivation in our daily actions, and gives us hope in our spirit. Here are several different translations of Proverbs 29:18, the benchmark scripture for vision.

"Where there is no vision, the people perish." (KJV)

"Where there is no vision (revelation), the people are unrestrained." (NASB)

"Where there is no revelation, the people cast off restraint." (NIV)

"Without revelation a nation fades, but it prospers in knowing the law." (FF)

"Without prophecy, the people become demoralized." (NAB)

The Power of Vision

Once vision is defined, it becomes a tool that is used to move an entire church into its future. Without the implementation of vision, people and churches perish. Leaders must provide clear vision to their flock.

Clear Vision Provides the Church _with clear direction_ .
"Where is this church going?" The answer to this question brings the future into focus and motivates all to become involved. As God's people, if we are to accomplish great things for God, we must know what it is we are trying to accomplish.

Clear Vision Enables the Church _to move together_ .
It is critical that a church advances together in unity of mind, spirit and purpose. When vision is regularly communicated, it serves as a constant reminder of what we as a team have agreed to pursue.

Clear Vision is the _lifeblood of motivation_ ***to the Church.***
It is the fuel that sustains a fire in the hearts of people. It motivates people to give their life, time and finances. Vision allows people to become involved based not on need, but upon the revelation of a church's direction.

As a committed congregation, we share a common dream and determination to accomplish our God-given vision. Our desire is to be an effective instrument of God. We will do this by building a local church in this region that is being restored to biblical pattern and power, which then becomes an instrument for Kingdom purposes. The result is a harvesting church that reaches out, brings in, and keeps the harvest, which is people.

Our Vision Statement

To move forward in unity as leaders, we must clearly understand the specific vision God has given our church.*

Our vision is:

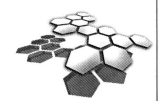

*See Appendix p.157 for City Bible Church's example.

Our Vision Values

Biblical values are the building blocks of our vision. Without these values, the vision would be nothing more than mere words. These values breathe life into the vision and sustain the quality of the vision.*

Our church values are:

*See Appendix p.157 for City Bible Church's example.

THE VISION OF SMALL GROUPS

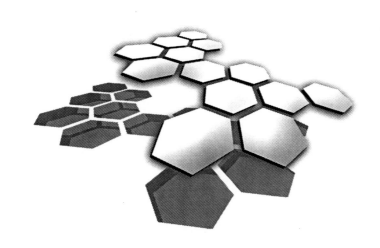

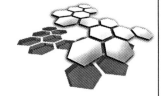

The Vision of Small Groups
Chapter Two

As we are committed to aligning our vision to biblical truths and values, it is imperative that we look at the biblical view of small groups as our template for building our small group ministry. Small groups are not a new method, but a biblical truth built on a firm Scriptural base. In fact, small groups have the greatest biblical support of all methods. Building on the foundation of God's Word allows us to honor our core values and build the church God's way, while withstanding and avoiding the storms of change brought about by the ongoing fads and ideas that rise up throughout church culture today.

As we continue to build the future of our church on the foundation of small groups, it is important that you as a leader appreciate and understand the rich biblical heritage you have and enjoy the ability to carry on this wonderful eternal plan.

The Biblical Foundation for Small Groups

Importance of Relationship _is established in the God-head_.
The concept of small groups is based around the nature of God. The Bible begins by launching this concept in Genesis 1:1, stating that God is our Creator and the Creator of all things. In this context, the name of God (*Elohīm*) is plural, not singular. This emphasizes the nature of relationships shown in the union of the Father, the Son, and the Holy Spirit. The Trinity (the essential nature of God) reveals to us the concept that God's desire is to see close relationships established.

Small Group Concept _Old Testament_.
Throughout the Old Testament we see the concept of small groups as they relate to God's people. From God's dealings with a complete nation, to a specific tribe, and then down to the family unit, the small group concept was implemented and embraced (see Genesis 50:8; Exodus 18, 40:38; Numbers 26:21-49; Joshua 13-22).

Small Group Concept in the Ministry _of Jesus_.
If there was ever an individual who modeled the importance and effectiveness of small groups, it would be Jesus himself. As stated by Neil McBride in his book *How to Lead Small Groups*, "For me, Jesus' involvement in a small group is the most convincing rationale for why local churches need to seriously consider including groups as an integral part of the congregational lives. While it may not be wise or even appropriate for believers to mimic Jesus' every act, such as healing a blind man by spitting on his eyes (see Mark 8:32), it is logical to replicate those behavioral patterns that constituted His methods of ministry. Therefore, it makes tremendous sense to explore Jesus' use of small groups."[1] Jesus demonstrated seven major principles using the small group concept.

1. He began His earthly ministry by forming a small group of disciples. (see Matthew 4:18-22; Luke 6:13-16).

2. He used small groups as His central method of establishing and building relationships (see Mark 3:14).

3. He spent more time with twelve men than all of humanity combined!

4. He had a balanced ministry focus between small group and large group ministry situations.

5. His small group teachings, relationships, and involvement were the platform for the effectiveness of his ministry in the secular world.

6. He used small groups as a means to impart truth, power, vision, and character.

7. He used small groups as a primary means of leadership training and multiplication (see Luke 8:10).

Small Group Concept in the *New Testament Church* .
The emphasis on small groups did not end with Jesus, but became the model for the New Testament church. From the very conception of the church in the book of Acts, small groups were the vehicles used to build the church and evangelize the world.

> *Acts 2:46-47 "So continuing daily with one accord in the temple, and breaking bread from **house to house,** they ate their food with gladness and simplicity of heart, praising God and having favor with all the people."*

> *Acts 5:42 "And daily in the temple, **and in every house,** they did not cease teaching and preaching Jesus as the Christ."*

> *Acts 20:20 "I kept back nothing that was helpful, but proclaimed it to you, and taught you publicly and from **house to house."***

Building a 21st Century New Testament Church
A local church must be founded upon, patiently moving in, and practicing the pattern and principles of New Testament divine order of what the church is to be. A New Testament church:

1. Is joined together to fulfill God's purposes.

2. Is committed to building strong families into a strong local church.

3. Is structured to a New Testament pattern.

4. Is expanding and impacting its neighborhoods, city and region.

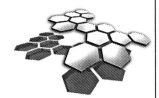

Fifteen Marks of a 21st Century New Testament Church

Acts 2-7 describes the first seven years of the church Christ built after His ascension. These chapters describe the culture of the Kingdom of God in terms of priorities and practices. As we move into our future, these are priorities for us as a people of God. Each point is critical to instill into every small group.

A _Powerful_ *Church*

Acts 1:8 "But you shall receive power when the Holy Spirit has come upon you; and you shall be witnesses to Me in Jerusalem, and in all Judea and Samaria, and to the end of the earth."

A _witnessing_ *Church*

Acts 1:8 "But you shall receive power when the Holy Spirit has come upon you; and you shall be witnesses to Me in Jerusalem, and in all Judea and Samaria, and to the end of the earth."

A _Praying_ *Church*

Acts 1:14 "These all continued with one accord in prayer and supplication, with the women and Mary the mother of Jesus, and with His brothers."

A _Unified_ *Church*

Acts 1:14 "These all continued with one accord in prayer and supplication, with the women and Mary the mother of Jesus, and with His brothers."

Acts 2:1 "Now when the Day of Pentecost had fully come, they were all with one accord in one place."

A _Sprit-filled_ *Church*

Acts 2:1-4 "Now when the Day of Pentecost had fully come, they were all with one accord in one place. And suddenly there came a sound from heaven, as of a rushing mighty wind, and it filled the whole house where they were sitting. Then there appeared to them divided tongues, as of fire, and one sat upon each of them. And they were all filled with the Holy Spirit and began to speak with other tongues, as the Spirit gave them utterance."

Acts 2:38 "Then Peter said to them, 'Repent, and let every one of you be baptized in the name of Jesus Christ for the remission of sins; and you shall receive the gift of the Holy Spirit.'"

A _Word / teaching_ *Church*

Acts 2:42 "And they continued steadfastly in the apostles' doctrine and fellowship, in the breaking of bread, and in prayers."

A _reverent_ *Church*

Acts 2:43 "Then fear came upon every soul, and many wonders and signs were done through the apostles."

A _Sharing_ *Church*

Acts 2:44-45 "Now all who believed were together, and had all things in common, and sold their possessions and goods, and divided them among all, as anyone had need."

A _gathering - together_ *Church*

Acts 2:44-45 "Now all who believed were together, and had all things in com-

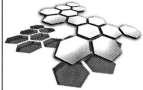

mon, and sold their possessions and goods, and divided them among all, as anyone had need."

A <u>Super natural</u> **Church**

Acts 2:2 "And suddenly there came a sound from heaven, as of a rushing mighty wind, and it filled the whole house where they were sitting."

Acts 19:11-12 "Now God worked unusual miracles by the hands of Paul, so that even handkerchiefs or aprons were brought from his body to the sick, and the diseases left them and the evil spirits went out of them."

A <u>fellowshipping</u> **Church**

Acts 2:46 "So continuing daily with one accord in the temple, and breaking bread from house to house, they ate their food with gladness and simplicity of heart."

A <u>rejoicing</u> **Church**

Acts 2:46 "So continuing daily with one accord in the temple, and breaking bread from house to house, they ate their food with gladness and simplicity of heart."

A <u>Worshipping</u> **Church**

Acts 2:47 "…praising God and having favor with all the people. And the Lord added to the church daily those who were being saved."

Acts 15:15-17 "And with this the words of the prophets agree, just as it is written: 'After this I will return and will rebuild the tabernacle of David, which has fallen down; I will rebuild its ruins, and I will set it up; so that the rest of mankind may seek the Lord, even all the Gentiles who are called by My name, says the Lord who does all these things.'"

An <u>appealing & relevant</u> **Church**

Acts 2:47 " …praising God and having favor with all the people. And the Lord added to the church daily those who were being saved."

A <u>Growing & expanding</u> **Church**

Acts 2:47 "…praising God and having favor with all the people. And the Lord added to the church daily those who were being saved."

Two Growth Factors of the New Testament Church

From the mandate given to the church in Acts 1:8, and the filling and releasing of the church in Acts 2, we see two factors which combine to produce rapid conversion growth.

Acts 2:41,47 "Then those who gladly received his word were baptized; and that day about three thousand souls were added to them…praising God and having favor with all the people. And the Lord added to the church daily those who were being saved."

Acts 4:4 "However, many of those who heard the word believed; and the number of the men came to be about five thousand."

Acts 5:14 "And believers were increasingly added to the Lord, multitudes of both men and women."

The rapid numerical growth threatened to undo the blessed success of the early church. Its quality could continue only if structural reorganization took place. The Jerusalem church became a meta-church, signifying both a change of mind about how ministry is to be done and a change of form in the infrastructure of the church. The following two growth factors are clearly seen as a model for us today.

Growth Factor #1: _The balanced heartbeat of the congregation and small groups_ .

As the church moved into a small group structure, the corporate gathering was not discarded. The small group became a means of supporting and strengthening the church as a whole.

> *Acts 2:46-47 "So continuing daily with one accord in the temple, and breaking bread from house to house, they ate their food with gladness and simplicity of heart, praising God and having favor with all the people. And the Lord added to the church daily those who were being saved."*

The Balance of Congregational Gathering and Small Groups

CONGRETATION Whole Church Gathering	**SMALL GROUPS** House to House
1. _____	1. _____
2. _____	2. _____
3. _____	3. _____
4. _____	4. _____
5. _____	5. _____
see 2 Chronicles 5:11-14; Acts 1:14, 2:1,41,44; Hebrews 10:24,25	see Matthew 28:19-20; Acts 20:20; Romans 14:7; Colossians 1:28-29; Hebrews 3:13; 1 John 3:14-18

Growth Factor #2: _____ .

As the necessity of discipling new converts continued to grow, and the needs in the church increased, it was critical to identify those who were gifted in leadership and release them to lead the church.

> *Acts 6:1-7 "Now in those days, when the number of the disciples was multiplying, there arose a murmuring against the Hebrews by the Hellenists, because their widows were neglected in the daily distribution. Then the twelve summoned the multitude of the disciples and said, 'It is not desirable that we should leave the word of God and serve tables. Therefore, brethren, seek out from among you seven men of good reputation, full of the Holy Spirit and wisdom, whom we may appoint over this business… Then the word of God spread, and the number of the disciples multiplied greatly in Jerusalem, and a great many of the priests were obedient to the faith."*

FOUR-FOLD PURPOSE OF SMALL GROUPS

1. _Relationships_

☑ Friendship development
☑ Honest sharing
☑ Community-belonging, acceptance
☑ Shared life; meals; time
☑ Accountability

#8

2. _Pastoral Care_

☑ Accepting and belonging
☑ Support
☑ Crisis help
☐ Counseling
☑ Supportive environment for struggle, change, and decision

3. _Equipping_

☑ Discovery and use of spiritual gifts
☑ Development of lay leadership
☑ Multiplication of groups and people
☐ Platform for Christian ministry
☑ Encouragement to become active, reproducing disciple of Christ

4. _Evangelism_

☐ Mobility and flexibility
☐ Informality
☐ Freedom
☑ Contagious faith
☑ Training in witnessing
☐ Strategic growth

#3

The Goals of Small Groups

We have established these goals for our small group ministry based upon the model of the church found in the New Testament and our expectation to see people establish relationships and be cared for, and for large growth to be added to our congregation, just as in the book of Acts. Although there are ten detailed goals listed below, each one is woven into the two main focal points of the small group ministry—healthy members and healthy small groups.

Healthy Member Profile

Healthy Small Group Profile

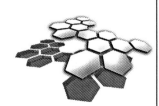

*See Appendix page 159 for City Bible Church's examples.

1. To see the harvest gathered, assimilated, and discipled.

2. To develop quality small group leaders who are prepared and equipped for a great harvest.

3. To train church members to assist in evangelizing and discipling.

4. To be a New Testament church which has a balanced emphasis on both the corporate gathering and the small group ministry.

5. To become a church with a multitude of small groups acting as home discipleship centers that multiply quickly and efficiently.

6. To assure every member of our church the highest level of care at the lowest level of structure. To provide each member of our church a personal pastoral touch, and ensure ongoing pastoral care.

7. To spread ministry responsibilities to other believers in the small group, utilizing them, but not overburdening any of them. To mobilize, motivate and equip each person for effective service recognizing their calling and gifting for service in the body of Christ.

8. To involve each member of our church in a small group, enabling them to build strong relationships within the church.

9. To ensure that a small group leader's scope of responsibility does not exceed their ability to provide effective care.

10. To promote and honor relationships over programs and methods. Relationships must become the central focus within a small group.

Defining Community

Each small group must build their foundation on the foundation of "community." In many small group ministry models, the focal point is on the meeting itself and not the developing and strengthening of body life all throughout the year. It is our intention to have a balanced focus of both community and meetings.

> **Community:** The intentional development of meaningful, long-lasting relationships, based on common biblical principles and purposes, resulting in each person having a sense of belonging, acceptance, and significance.

Meeting Focus: directs most all energy and attention on the small group meeting itself, and minimizes any other "small group life" during the time in between meetings. This hinders the development of all aspects of relationships, leadership development, etc.

Community Focus: greatly increases the depth of relationships, and provides much opportunity for pastoral care, mentoring, leadership development, and creates true Acts 2 koinōnia all week long. Many other informal, natural contacts and encounters take place during the week. Those that have emphasized this as their foundation are the healthiest small groups in the church.

Advantages of Small Groups

As we build our future in small group ministry, we are ensured of reaping the benefits of this biblical form of reaching the lost and pastoring God's people. Here are some advantages of small groups:

1. Small groups are an effective means of rapidly reaching lost people in all regions of the city.

2. Small groups encourage evangelism to be practiced by every member.

3. Small groups provide a framework to bring practical, consistent and systematic growth in the lives of those under your care.

4. Small groups provide an atmosphere where people can be blessed by relationships regardless of the size of the church membership.

5. Small groups provide an opportunity for people to use their gifts and serve others, without being limited by the ministry opportunities in the corporate gathering.

6. Small groups allow each person to bear another's burden and assist in meeting the everyday needs of their brother and sister in Christ.

7. Small groups provide a framework for counseling and accountability.

8. Small groups provide a haven of security and refuge.

9. Small groups are a training ground for future leadership in small group ministry.

[1] Neil F. McBride, *How to Lead Small Groups*, NavPress, 1990, p.15

THE SMALL
GROUP NETWORK

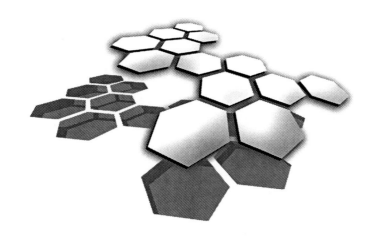

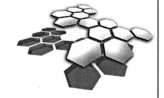

The Small Group Network
Chapter Three

In the book of Exodus, we find the account of Moses and his challenge to take care of the overwhelming needs of the children of Israel. He was a very gifted and anointed leader, but also a very burned-out and frustrated leader. Through the intervention of his father-in-law, Jethro, Moses was presented with a God-given structure that allowed him to handle the responsibility of pastoring and caring for over three million people.

The principles given to Moses in Exodus 18 consisted of breaking the multitudes into groups of tens, fifties, hundreds, and thousands. Moses moved into the role of showing the children of Israel how to live and what duties they were to perform. Moses then spent time training and appointing individuals for different levels of leadership.

As we continue to pursue our God-given vision of reaching our region for Christ, there must be a structure in place that allows us to pastor every person God brings our way. We realize every person matters to God, and the larger we become, the smaller we must be in our pastoral structure and care.

To better understand the information provided for you in this manual, it would help to know the overall structure of the small group ministry and the overall church. This is not an exhaustive explanation of the structure, duties and functions of each position, but a simple overview, so that you may better understand the relationships between each position.

Our Church Small Group Structure
Draw a diagram of your small group structure as shown by the class leader.*

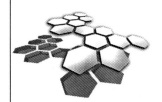

*See Appendix page 160 for City Bible Church's example.

Defining Ministry Positions

The small group structure is made up of many people; each one providing their area of gifting and expertise. Every person is important to the overall success of the small group ministry.

Write down the positions and a brief description of the different positions and their responsibilities concerning the small group ministry as defined by your class leader.*

*See Appendix page 161 for City Bible Church's example.

Types of Small Groups

While vision, values, and philosophy remain the same, focus and content may vary from group to group. The following list gives some examples of the types of small groups available in our church.*

*See Appendix page 169 for City Bible Church's examples.

THE MAKING OF A SMALL GROUP LEADER

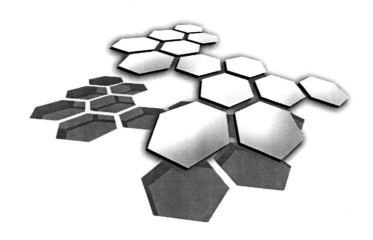

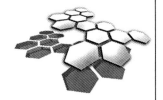

The Making of a ~~Small~~ *Community* Group Leader
Chapter Four

The development of the small group leader should be an important ministry within the church. Without quality leaders, it is extremely difficult to shepherd, train, and release the large number of people who are a part of the church. Effective leadership is essential.

As we labor together in building a 21st Century, New Testament church, our first priority must be to reproduce leaders with the same spirit, mind, and focus. This, in turn, will allow those we lead to receive the same spiritual gene, and ultimately reproduce these same traits in those they will lead (1 Timothy 2:2).

There is a certain element of leadership that is God-given and totally outside of one's control. God does much of the calling and gifting that is necessary to be involved in a certain ministry. Yet it is also true that certain things can be cultivated by the called person, which will render him or her more fit for the task of God's choosing. Any leader who desires to excel in the small group ministry must give attention to areas of development that will bring great success and fruit.

Each small group leader should make an ongoing commitment and maintain a balance in four main areas:

1. Commitment to God

2. Commitment to Yourself and Family

3. Commitment to the Church

4. Commitment to the People

Say

Commitment to God
Small group leaders are servants of God who communicate the truth of God by leading people in evangelism, shepherding, spiritual growth and reproduction. As a small group leader, you model the Christian life to others by first showing your commitment to God.

 Read

A _____*Called*_____ **Leader**

Leaders know they have been called because deep in their hearts lies a burden to care for and lead others. They see others as Christ did, people who are hurting and in need of a shepherd who will protect, provide, and strengthen them for the journey ahead.

> *1 Thessalonians 2:8 "So, affectionately longing for you, we were well pleased to impart to you not only the gospel of God, but also our own lives, because you had become dear to us."*

> *1 Peter 5:2-3 "Shepherd the flock of God which is among you, serving as overseers, not by compulsion but willingly, not for dishonest gain but eagerly; nor as being lords over those entrusted to you, but being examples to the flock."*

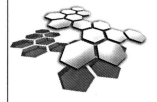

where are
You spiritually
w/ the Lord?
It's based on
how much time ✻
You're spending w/
God. Are
You growing in as
a follower of Jesus Christ?

Real ➝ ✻

A **Spiritual** *Leader*

Small group leaders must demonstrate their maturity as a spiritual leader. This leadership trait is birthed by spending time with God, coupled with proper grooming from Godly leadership. 1 Timothy 5:22 speaks of not giving too much responsibility too soon, which is an important principle in selecting small group leaders.

A **growing** *Leader*

The goal of every leader is to become a total follower of Jesus Christ. Although leaders are not expected to be perfect, there should be a desire to be growing toward that goal. If you are to model spiritual growth and maturity and encourage others along the same path, it must first be present in your own life.

*2 Peter 3:18 "But **grow in the grace and knowledge** of our Lord and Savior Jesus Christ. To Him be the glory both now and forever. Amen."*

*Colossians 1:28 "Him we preach, warning every man and teaching every man in all wisdom, that we may present **every man perfect in Christ Jesus.**"*

*Ephesians 4:13 "till we all come to the unity of the faith and of the knowledge of the Son of God, **to a perfect man, to the measure of the stature of the fullness of Christ.**"*

Are you praying?
How's your prayer
life?

✗ A **praying** *Leader*

As a small group leader, prayer is your primary tool to become an effective leader. There are five main areas that should be a part of your regular prayer life.

1. Personal Prayer (see 1 Timothy 2:8).

2. Corporate Prayer (see Acts 2:42).

3. Prayer for Your Leaders (see 1 Timothy 2:2).

4. Prayer for Those You Lead (see Philippians 1:4,9; Colossians 1:3,9; Philemon 4).

5. Prayer for Specific Needs (see James 5:13-16).

A **Godly** *Leader*

The leadership of this church has the highest commitment to character and integrity. The gifts of the Spirit are greatly diminished if one lacks the character to administrate them. You represent Christ, His Church and His Cause! A commitment to Godly leadership is a sure ingredient to long-term success in your ministry position.

1. Commit yourself to being daily transformed, not conformed (see Romans 12:1-2; Philippians 1:9-10).

2. Commit yourself to developing Godly character (see 1 Thessalonians 2: 7-8; 1 Peter 5:1-4).

Commitment to Yourself and Your Family

A great leader begins by being a great family person. Whether you are married or single, living at home or on your own, this principle still applies. Leading must first begin in the home. There should never be a time where your ministry is more important than your family.

Should never

As a small group leader, you should strive to keep the following leadership characteristics an active part of your life.

A ___Family___ ***Leader***

The greatest disciples you will ever build are your own family. Heads of households can apply this principle to their spouse and children. Younger small group leaders can even apply this to their siblings. The most successful small group leaders are the ones who apply all of these leadership principles to their families.

1 Timothy 3:4-5 "... one who rules his own house well, having his children in submission with all reverence (for if a man does not know how to rule his own house, how will he take care of the church of God?)."

Read

It is imperative that you learn to balance the pressures of leading a small group and your time with your family. There are times that may require an extra night out, or some extra time in a counseling situation, but make sure to always balance these times with extra time with your family.

A ___Prudent___ ***Leader***

Someone once said, "Success is ninety percent time management." This statement is fairly accurate! Often those things which are urgent and tend to consume our time are hardly important; and those things which are very important, rarely get our attention. The Bible advises us to "redeem the time." Having the necessary time to properly lead a small group is an important qualification. Burnout is one of the biggest reasons that leaders quit ministering.

> *Colossians 4:5 "Walk in wisdom toward those who are outside, **redeeming the time.**" (RSV states, "making the most of the time")*

*Ephesians 5:16-17 "**redeeming the time,** because the days are evil. Therefore do not be unwise, but understand what the will of the Lord is."*

→ Read

Most people would assume that they do not have the time to do an adequate job in leading. However, upon closer examination of their schedule, the reality would be that they don't do an adequate job of managing their schedule. The problem is usually not a shortage of time but how available time is used.

Read

Larry Stockstill, Senior Pastor of Bethany World Prayer Center in Louisiana, has a great illustration concerning the prioritizing of our time.

> *"Our most important values are like big rocks that we are trying to put in a large pickle jar. If the jar is already filled with sand, gravel, and water (other less important activities), we are not going to be able to put the big rocks into the jar. But if we put the big rocks in first, then the sand, gravel, and water will fit in between the spaces. Regardless of what goes in, the key is to put in the big rocks first."[1]*

Below are ten life-saving tips to help in making you a successful small group leader.

1. Find a time management system that works best for your needs (Day Timer, Day Runner, Palm, iPAQ, Outlook, etc.).

2. Determine your priorities and goals and schedule them first as far in advance as possible (work, family, church, and ministry).

3. Know how and where you spend your time and eliminate any time-wasters.

4. Learn the art of saying, "No!" You are to give your time, not allow others to rob your time.

5. Identify tasks that are similar and group them together to accomplish at the same time.

6. Identify tasks that can be delegated and *delegate them!* Use this as opportunity to raise other leaders and potential leaders within your small group.

7. Schedule all small group meetings and training sessions for the year.

8. Determine the time that is needed in order to study for your small group meeting and to call your people weekly, and schedule these in.

9. Keep your time management system with you at all times. Make sure not to overbook yourself.

10. Stay in contact with your spouse and/or family members to discuss any additional items that will conflict with your existing schedule.

Commitment to the Church

A leader who is committed to God must build the Kingdom of God, not the kingdom of self. You must have this truth lodged deep within the fabric of your being. A small group leader is to continually work on developing the following leadership qualities into their lives.

A _____ Team _____ Leader

Teamwork in leadership is essential. Using one's God-given gifts together with the rest of the Body is the pattern for building the church (see Romans 12:4-18). There must be a conviction that places Christ and His people above all of your own desires, ambitions and opinions. A team leader must see the ministry as a way to serve and give rather than a way to fulfill and promote themselves.

> Romans 12:16-18 "Be of the same mind toward one another. Do not set your mind on high things, but associate with the humble. Do not be wise in your own opinion. Repay no one evil for evil. Have regard for good things in the sight of all men. If it is possible, as much as depends on you, live peaceably with all men."

A _____ Servant _____ Leader

Leading is serving and should be the motivation for every small group leader. It was said of Jesus that He came to serve, not to be served. Servanthood stems from knowing who you are in Christ, and not what position you are trying to attain

Talk, and representing the church.
Taming the tongue.
Pastor spk on this last week,

in order to build your own identity and ministry. This is simply put in Galatians 5:13, *"Through love serve one another."*

Here is a great poem taken from Larry Stockstill's *301 Leader's Training Manual.*

> *The secure are into towels…*
> *The insecure are into titles.*
>
> *The secure are people conscious…*
> *The insecure are position conscious.*
>
> *The secure want to add value to others…*
> *The insecure want to receive value from others.*[2]

A Supportive **Leader**

A supportive leader will always be willing to accept any assignment necessary to advance the team's overall vision. This is shown through rejecting a position-conscious attitude. A supportive Leader becomes great by making others great! At all times, a small group leader needs to be supportive of the vision and direction charted by the senior pastor and leadership team of the church.

A Committed **Leader**

Being a committed leader is understanding that reaching, shepherding, and train-ing people requires hard work and a commitment to the process. You must under-stand the difference between a "commitment over convenience" attitude and an "I'll do whatever it takes to get the job done" attitude.

A committed leader is also available. Availability is the necessary ingredient to be-ing a useful vessel to God, to other leaders, and to those whom you serve. Being available requires good discipline of time and priorities. Priscilla and Aquilla were leaders who lived these principles.

> *Romans 16:3-4 "Greet Priscilla and Aquilla, my fellow workers in Christ Jesus, who risked their own necks for my life, to whom not only I give thanks, but also all the churches of the Gentiles."*

A Facilitating **Leader** ✗ *Revd*

A facilitator is one who coaches, not one who controls. An effective small group leader will always be looking for ways to make it easier for others to succeed. These truths should apply to every small group meeting!
A facilitating leader will:

1. Make it easier for others to find meaningful relationships.

2. Make it easier for all the needs of the small group to be met.

3. Make it easier for people to find their place of service.

4. Make it easier for people to identify with the corporate vision of the church.

5. Make it easier for people to grow to maturity in Christ.

A Giving **Leader**

Commitment to the church can always be measured by the giving to the church. Those who are committed to something are willing to support it at all costs! Every small group leader is to be committed to supporting the church through their *tithes and offerings*. It is impossible to ask others whom you are leading to support the church when your own lifestyle does not set the example.

Matthew 6:21 "For where your treasure is, there your heart will be also."

Commitment to People

A small group leader should understand that the goal is not to build a great program, but to build great people. The reason we are building a church is because people matter to God, and they matter to us. A small group leader not only needs to be committed to God and the leadership of the Church, but also to those they are trying to reach and shepherd.

A_____Shepherd_____ *Leader*

A shepherd leader gives his life for the sheep. We understand that a shepherd takes care of the needs of the flock and protects them from any intrusion.

Acts 20:28 "Therefore take heed to yourselves and to all the flock, among which the Holy Spirit has made you overseers, to shepherd the church of God which He purchased with His own blood."

John 10:11-12 "I am the good shepherd. The good shepherd gives His life for the sheep. But a hireling, he who is not the shepherd, one who does not own the sheep, sees the wolf coming and leaves the sheep and flees; and the wolf catches the sheep and scatters them."

As small group leaders, your desire should be to follow the example of Jesus as the Good Shepherd. Listed below are seven areas where we are to focus our shepherding ministry.

1. Care for all the needs of the flock (see Psalms 23:1; Jeremiah 23:4).

2. Raise up strong marriages, families, singles, and future families (see Malachi 4:6).

3. Bring each person to a place of personal maturity, including reaching and discipling the lost (see Ephesians 4:13, Matthew 28:19-20).

4. Develop and maintain strong interpersonal relationships, which create a sense of community (see Ephesians 4:16).

5. Assist and equip each person in finding and fulfilling their place of ministry in the church, resulting in spiritual reproduction of every believer (see Ephesians 4:11-12).

6. Be available to each person in your small group for counseling, support, encouragement, and comfort (see Psalms 23:3).

7. Lead by example, and encourage others to gather the lost into your small group (see Ezekiel 34:12-16).

A ___Confidential___ **Leader** ✗

Those whom you lead must feel they can trust you with any situation. Those in your small group must feel confident that you will protect them and their interests. A small group leader should follow these four principles.

1. Protect sensitive information. Don't be guilty of sins of the tongue:
    Talebearing (see Leviticus 19:16)
    Backbiting (see Proverb 25:23)
    Gossip (see Deuteronomy 5:20)
    Whispering (see Romans 1:29)
    Slander (see Psalm 101:5)

2. Love others continually. Always seek the interest of others over your own interests. (see Proverbs 10:12; 17:19).

3. Remain loyal and faithful (see Proverbs 11:13).

4. Build others up; do not tear them down (see Ephesians 4:29-30).

A ___Personal___ **Leader**

The success of your small group will be measured by the depth of your relationships with those you lead. Leadership impact is measured in relationship authenticity and not from an official title of oversight. Jesus always ministered to the individual and their need showing them they were very important to Him (see John 4:5-30; 8:1-11).

A ___Capable___ **Leader**

A capable leader desires to serve others and do whatever it takes to accomplish the task. Being capable for the task is having the time, energy and resources necessary to fulfill the need. An inventory may be needed to remove unnecessary commitments and distractions so that you have the spiritual, emotional and physical energy to accomplish God's calling on your life.

A ___Courageous___ **Leader**   ✳

Joshua was a leader with courageous faith. He was always ready for the challenge at hand. He understood that the Lord was with him in every situation and as long as he remained courageous and filled with faith and not fear, the Lord would be by his side.

You must show courage to those you lead. There are times where you must step out in faith to lead others (prayer, evangelism, counseling, etc.) and pave the way for them to follow (see Joshua 1:6-7,9,18; 2:11; 3:15; 10:25; 14:7-11; 17:17-18; 23:6; 24:23).   *Read*

A ___Gracious___ **Leader**   ✳ *Read*

A gracious leader is one who understands true leadership versus domineering leadership. On one hand, a leader is not to allow anyone to take advantage of a situation and walk all over them. On the other hand, they are not to control every person and cause long-lasting paralysis. Here are a few characteristics.

A gracious leader:

1. Concentrates on influencing by encouragement, inspiration and motivation.

2. Enjoys a good relationship with co-workers, showing respect for individuals.

3. Works with others toward achieving long-range goals and being concerned for others' development.

4. Aims to make himself unnecessary.

5. Encourages others, versus condemning others.

6. Shares in the accomplishment instead of taking all the credit.

7. Is always willing to discuss actions instead of just taking action alone.

8. Desires to equip and train others that will far exceed himself.

Here is a comparison between a gracious leader and a controlling leader:

Gracious Leader	Controlling Leader
Coaches people	Drives people
Depends on good will	Depends on authority
Inspires enthusiasm	Inspires fear
Says, "We did it!"	Says, "I did it!"
Fixes the breakdown	Blames for the breakdown
Shows how it's done	Tells how it's done
Says, "Let's go!"	Says, "Go!"

A ____Harvest____ Leader

Every Christian has been called to the ministry of reconciliation (see 2 Corinthians 5:18). One of the primary responsibilities, not only of the Christian, but especially of the small group leader, is to reach lost people. We are His ambassadors, and He is making His appeal through us. Leading others in evangelism is the way your small group and the church will grow in reaching your city for Christ.

1 Peter 3:15 "But sanctify the Lord God in your hearts, and always be ready to give a defense to everyone who asks you a reason for the hope that is in you, with meekness and fear."

2 Corinthians 5:18 "Now all things are of God, who has reconciled us to Himself through Jesus Christ, and has given us the ministry of reconciliation."

2 Corinthians 5:20-21 "Now then, we are ambassadors for Christ, as though God were pleading through us: we implore you on Christ's behalf, be reconciled to God. For He made Him who knew no sin to be sin for us, that we might become the righteousness of God in Him."

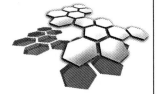

A _____*Reproducing*_____ ***Leader***

The success of a small group is not measured in the size of the meeting but in the ability to reproduce itself on a regular basis. There are many parallels between natural parenting and spiritual parenting, both ending in the goal of reproduction. One of the most important commitments we can make to the people we serve is to encourage them to be active, healthy, *reproducing* members of the local church.

[1] Bethany World Church Pastors, *Small Group Leader Training 301*, (Bethany World Prayer Center, 1998)

[2] Ibid.

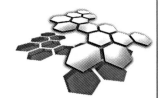

THE REQUIREMENTS OF A SMALL GROUP LEADER

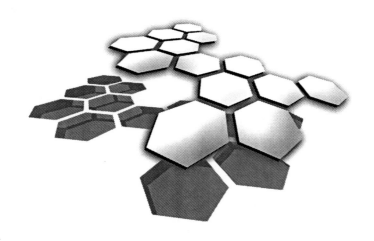

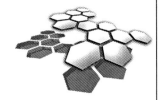

The Requirements of a Small Group Leader
Chapter Five

Small group leaders are meant to be an extension of the pastoral and harvest ministry of the local church. The ministry of a small group leader involves shepherding, caring, loving, strengthening, encouraging, reaching out, watching over, and supporting those entrusted to your care. Small group leaders are the arms of the vision of the church and assist the senior pastor and other church leadership of the church in fulfilling their ministry to the body.

Small Group Leader Ministry Description
The small group leader will help facilitate the vision of the church by creating a sense of ongoing community and meeting regularly with their small group. They will be responsible for all organization, planning and shepherding of the flock given to their care. The small group leader will raise up other potential leaders in the group and mentor them in leading their own small group. The small group leader will lead the small group in making an impact on the lives of those who don't know Christ as well as being involved in reaching out to their neighborhoods by bringing the good news of Jesus Christ.

Requirements and Qualifications of a Small Group Leader
Listed below are requirements and qualifications necessary to become a small group leader.

_____

_____

_____

_____

_____

_____

* See Appendix page 167 for City Bible Church's example.

Responsibilities of a Small Group Leader

There are eight main areas of responsibility for a small group leader.

Be _____ in your small group.
As a small group leader, your goal is to know the condition of everyone in your group. Proverbs 27:23 says, "Be diligent to know the state of your flocks, and attend to your herds."

❑ Memorize and know the names of every person in your small group, including children.

❑ Keep close communication so that you know how they are doing spiritually, emotionally, physically, domestically, and financially.

❑ Focus on building community within your small group, which provides a sense of belonging, acceptance and significance for every person that is a part of your small group.

Be an _____ that your small group can follow.
You may have heard from your parents at one time, "Do as I say, not as I do!" This statement is great to use at a point where you are embarrassed by your actions, but it doesn't work in real life. Paul focuses on six specific areas in writing to Timothy,

1 Timothy 4:12 "Be an example to the believers in word, in conduct, in love, in spirit, in faith, in purity."

Review the following six areas and ask yourselves the accompanying questions.

❑ **"Word"**   Does your speech betray you? What is in your daily conversation?

❑ **"Lifestyle"**   Do your actions follow your convictions and confessions?

❑ **"Love"**   Do you continually display acts of kindness and compassion?

❑ **"Spirit"**   Do you sense freedom and liberty in your daily life?

❑ **"Faith"**   Do you look at the glass as half empty or half full?

❑ **"Purity"**   Are you continually confronting areas of sin and shortcomings?

Reach out to _____ into your small group.
The small group is not to be just a place in which we pastor and care for the needs of the people in the church, but also a tool for reaching spiritual seekers in our city. Jesus himself left the ninety-nine to go after the one that was lost. It is stated in Matthew 18:11, "For the Son of Man has come to save that which was lost." As followers of Christ, we must encourage our small group members to be motivated and fruitful in this critical ministry of the church. As small group leaders we should:

❑ Be a witness in daily life. Evangelism is who we are, not just what we do!

❑ Look for creative ways in which the group can be effective in reaching relatives, friends, neighbors, and co-workers, both in and outside of the small group meetings.

❑ Be actively involved in all church-related, and other ministry-sponsored outreach events.

❑ Be on the lookout for people who are new or unattached at the corporate services and invite them to your group. This would include ministering at the altar, meeting people in the foyer, or keeping an eye out for new people attending.

❑ Work closely and promptly with the church leadership in following up any names given to you for your small group.

❑ Be aggressive in keeping the "back door" closed by calling everyone in your small group regularly and giving special attention to anyone who is not regularly attending your small group.

Minister _____ in your small group.
Each person attending your small group will have his or her own special blend of needs. Some may be faced with a crisis situation involving a physical, emotional or financial disaster while others may have needs which require some ongoing pastoral care. Regardless of the type of needs, your function is to assist each person into becoming a healthy, active, reproducing member of the church!

A small group leader should evaluate the people in the small group
In order to maintain a healthy small group, there are some questions that should be considered frequently .

❑ What are their most pressing physical needs?

❑ What are their most pressing spiritual needs?

❑ How can I best address and assist in meeting these needs?

❑ What do I feel are these persons' strengths, and where can I see them functioning and using their spiritual gifts in the small group and in the Church?

❑ How can I help them develop their gifts and become effective in service?

❑ What is their financial status? Do they tithe? Do they have a budget? Can I help them in becoming financially free?

❑ Is their marriage strong? How do they treat their children? Can I assist in strengthening their family?

❑ Do they attend church regularly? Do they attend small group regularly? Are they involved in any other church ministries or functions of the church?

A small group leader should counsel people in the group
Once you have evaluated your people, you will probably find areas of need that should be addressed. Some situations may need some form of instruction and guidance. Here are some recommendations for situations that require some form of counsel.

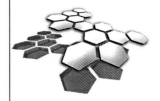

❑ Schedule a consistent time (only as needed) in your calendar when you can focus on meeting with people who need additional care. Use it as an opportunity to eat a meal together, as well as to build relationship with the individual(s) you are ministering to.

❑ Take an opportunity to meet with people before, between, or after a weekend service.

❑ Spend time reading *Common Care Counseling* by Christian Equippers International[1] to sharpen your counseling skills and deal with common-care situations.

❑ Get involved in any other training offered by the church, or read recommended counseling materials.

❑ Identify the problem and determine if the situation requires the further support of other church leadership. Some cases may need to be turned over to more qualified or experienced church leaders. This will be further explained in the "Pastoral Care and the Small Group" chapter.

❑ Keep your immediate leadership supervisor informed of every situation, regardless of how small the situation may be.

A small group leader should visit small group members who are sick
If there are people who are in your group who become ill, be sure to give them additional attention and care.

❑ Call them and pray for God to heal them.

❑ See if they have any special needs and assist the group in meeting them.

❑ Determine if special meals are necessary.

❑ Visit them if they are hospitalized.

Foster the _____ within the group.
One of the main reasons people stay in a local church is relationships. The number one reason people leave churches is a lack of relationships. The development and maintenance of healthy, long-lasting relationships is essential in building a healthy small group and a healthy local church. This is the foundational core to building community within your small group. Here are some tips to assist you in developing meaningful relationships:

❑ Plan a time of fellowship at every meeting. Encourage everyone to participate in the refreshments and visiting.

❑ Plan activities that cause individuals to open up to each other and share their lives with one another.

❑ Have open discussions in the group and encourage everyone to discuss the topic. Make sure to draw out those who are quieter.

❑ Encourage the people in your group to get involved with each other during the week outside the group meetings. As the leader, you should practice this principle with your people.

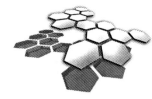

❑ Plan occasional group "getaways" where you go somewhere for the day or for the weekend.

❑ Create an "adopt-a-friend" in your group that encourages people to pray for each other.

❑ Plan special men's or women's activities who bring a special time of bonding.

Raise up and _____ in areas of ministry.
Your small group is a great place to train future leaders in the Kingdom of God. Each week there are many tasks that need to be accomplished, and you should be looking for people within your small group to assist in the tasks.

People want to feel that they belong to something. They want to feel important. They want to feel that they have value. Look for possibilities to create ministry opportunities for every person in your group. It may be as simple as overseeing refreshments, assisting with the children, making copies or phone calls. Whatever the task may be, mobilize your people and create some ownership within your group! Here are some tips to assist you in mobilizing your people.

❑ Make a commitment to use the **Personal Growth Chart** in planning every group meeting.

❑ Make a list of every potential ministry opportunity in your group.

❑ Consider the strength, gifts, maturity, and commitment of each person in your group.

❑ Meet regularly with your assistant and potential leaders to discuss plans for the group. This will give you the opportunity to mentor those under you, as well as discuss mobilizing others to perform the regular functions associated with your small group meeting.

❑ As the Holy Spirit directs you, look for ways to encourage and enlist people to use their gifts in the group.

❑ Recognize that every person has a place to function.
(see 1 Corinthians 12)

❑ If you have families in your small group, don't overlook children and teenagers. Give them a place to serve as well.

❑ Be on the constant lookout for future leaders, assistants, and hosts, so you may continually reproduce yourself and plant new groups.

Create a _____ in your small group.
The larger a church becomes, the smaller it must become! A small group is the key tool in creating long-lasting relationships. As your group deepens in maturity, your small group will feel more like a family. This is very similar to fostering meaningful relationships within the small group, but moves the relational base from an individual focus to an overall group focus. Relationships can be healthy between individuals but poor among the group. The group leader should work to strengthen both!

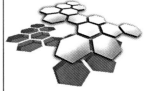

There is a balance between spending time with your immediate family and with those in your small group. As you strive to find the balance that best fits you and your family, look for ways of creating a family atmosphere between your family and your small group.

> *Philippians 1:7-8 "Just as it is right for me to think this of you all, **because I have you in my heart**, inasmuch as both in my chains and in the defense and confirmation of the gospel, **you all are partakers with me** of grace. For God is my witness, how greatly **I long for you** all with the affection of Jesus Christ."*

Here are some quick tips to assist you in creating a family atmosphere.

❑ Encourage everyone to pray for each other regularly.

❑ Encourage everyone to get involved relationally with each other on a regular basis outside of the small group meeting.

❑ Invite different individuals or families over once a month for dinner.

❑ Do special activities with each other such as child's sports games, the beach, a picnic, etc.

❑ Encourage everyone to send others a note or card for their birthday, anniversary, Christmas, or to encourage them.

_____ ***your small group regularly.***
In order to reach your community with the gospel of Jesus Christ, as well as keep up with the growing number of people coming into the church, there must be an aggressive plan to reproduce small groups on a consistent basis. You are a part of this God-given strategy.

One of the primary ingredients to a healthy small group is raising up and releasing leaders. At any given time you may be working with a few assistants, molding and shaping them into birthing your next small group. Although there is an entire section of this manual that addresses this issue, here are some basic thoughts to consider:

❑ View yourself as a reproducer and small group planter.

❑ Always be working with an assistant and potential leaders with the intention of sending them out to plant their own small group.

❑ Keep looking for new potential leaders and begin shaping them into your future assistants.

❑ Keep the vision of "small group planting" in the minds of your people by discussing it regularly in your small group meeting. It is a part of their "small group gene."

❑ Don't allow your group to react with apprehension regarding the multiplication of your group. Some may not want to see those they are close to leave to start another group. However, encourage them that relationships supersede the boundaries of a regular meeting. They can continue to be close friends even if they attend different groups. Plant the vision of multiplication early and maintain it continually to prevent dissatisfaction or

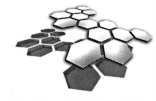

apprehension.

❑ Encourage every assistant and any future leaders to attend the small group leaders training course and any other church-required training, so they are trained and equipped to be released.

[1] To order the highly recommended *Common Care Counseling Handbook*, contact CEI at 1-800-662-0909.

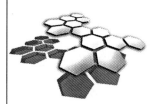

THE MULTIPLICATION OF THE SMALL GROUP

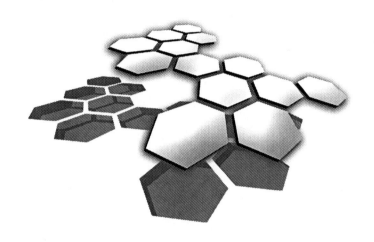

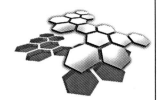

The Multiplication of the Small Group
Chapter Six

One of the most famous men in history, one who was responsible for shaping the history of mankind made this profound statement, "Give me a handful of young dedicated men who will give me their lives and I will control the world." He did just that! In 1903, he had seventeen followers. By 1918, he had 40,000 followers controlling over 160,000,000 people. In less than sixty years he impacted one-third of the planet. His name was Lenin! This man had a revelation of the power of multiplication. He built his empire on the philosophy of communism, which had a negative impact on the world using the same principle instituted by God!

The Principle of Multiplication

For years, the term "multiplication" has raised more questions than answers. Many have associated the term to stale, modern-day techniques that bypass relationships in order to obtain the goal of big numbers. However, upon closer examination of the word in its biblical context, this perception couldn't be further from the truth.

The word "multiply" was one of the original commands established by God to man in the first of nine covenants[1], the Edenic Covenant. This same command then resurfaces as God establishes the Abrahamic Covenant with man. In both scriptural references, as well as many others, the emphasis of multiplication was primarily targeted towards the family unit. The call was to establish healthy, strong, godly relationships and teach others to do likewise, resulting in a contagious, continual process that would spread the seed to all four corners of the globe! The reward would be a legacy and heritage for every person and generation. It is in the family where the greatest of relationships are established.

> *Genesis 1:28 "Then God blessed them, and God said to them, "**Be fruitful and multiply;** fill the earth and subdue it; have dominion over the fish of the sea, over the birds of the air, and over every living thing that moves on the earth."*

> *Genesis 22:17 "blessing I will bless you, **and in multiplying I will multiply** your descendants as the stars of the heaven and as the sand which is on the seashore; and your descendants shall possess the gate of their enemies."*

The Method of Multiplication _____.

Jesus himself modeled this biblical truth in His ministry on earth. In His last words to His disciples He didn't say, "Go and make decisions" but, "Go and make disciples." That means, make "healthy, active, reproducing members of the body of Christ!" Jesus was the perfect equipper. Of all the options possible to build His church, He chose twelve raw recruits. He then spent more time with the twelve than all of humanity combined. He devoted three and half years concentrating on reproducing himself into the individuals who would later change the world!

> *Matthew 28:19 "Go therefore and **make disciples** of all the nations, baptizing them in the name of the Father and of the Son and of the Holy Spirit."*

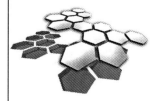

Jesus followed a very methodical plan of raising new leaders. From the first contact with His disciples until the final meeting before His ascension, these principles are seen. (See Mark 3:7-14; Luke 6:12, 17-19)

Jesus' Method	*Principle Learned*
I teach, you listen	Preparation
I do, you watch	Observation
I do, you help	Cooperation
You do, I help	Application
You do, I watch	Delegation
You do, I'm gone	Multiplication

The Sequence Jesus Used to _____.

The principle and methods used by Christ moved in a strategic sequence. These four main steps are what He used to multiply the message of the Gospel to the ends of the earth.

Step One: _____.

He spent many months searching and observing those in the crowds. When He saw those whom He would choose, He put out the plea, "Come! Follow me." (see Luke 5).

Step Two: _____.

He spent the first stage of their relationship training the disciples in the ministry of the Kingdom. His first phase of ministry was primarily solo acts, with the disciples observing and learning (see Mark 3:7-14).

Step Three: _____.

Once they were trained, He began to use them in ministry situations, and ultimately sent them out to become agents of the gospel message (see Luke 10).

Step Four: _____.

When He communicated His plans to leave, He commanded them to take the calling, training and sending to the lost, and reproduce themselves throughout the earth (see Acts 1:8).

Multiplication Promotes Fruitful Relationships

These principles of Jesus can be applied to us, His Church, today. The Church is God's spiritual family. God never intended that the extension and growth of the kingdom be without relationships, but through relationships! Those within the Church are our existing family, and those who have not yet come to Christ are our children, the blessing of the Lord.

It is through building strong relationships that we are able to earn the trust and respect to fix broken lives and make them strong, healthy Christians, so that they, in turn, might do likewise. Those that we reach, love, and build relationships with become our family and inheritance. Paul encourages the church in Thessalonica with this revelation of receiving their inheritance at the coming of the Lord Jesus. He understood that his hope, his joy and crown were those that he had reached with the gospel and then shaped them to become reproducing.

1 Thessalonians 2:19-20 "For what is our hope, or joy, or crown of rejoicing? Is it not even you in the presence of our Lord Jesus Christ at His coming? For you are our glory and joy."

There is a tension that has existed in the body of Christ for centuries. Two opposing views have surfaced that were never intended to conflict with one another, but to compliment each other. Those two views are caring for the people of God, and reaching the lost of the world.

Jesus made it clear through the Great Commission that both elements were to be instrumental in the foundation of His Church. He said in Matthew 28:19 "Go therefore and make disciples of all the nations." He did not say, "Go and preach the gospel only." Nor did He say, "Just make disciples." He said both! These two commands should create a cyclical process of building the Church—and through it the world is reached. We are to shepherd and strengthen those that God has entrusted to us and teach them to reach the lost. The lost, in turn, come to Christ and are shepherded and strengthened, so that they also reach the lost. Through this continual process, multiplication occurs and the Great Commission is fulfilled.

Small group church analyst Joel Comiskey states,

Try to grasp the bigger picture that small group reproduction draws. To multiply a group, a leader must pray daily for small group members, prepare himself spiritually before God, visit the members regularly, make numerous phone calls to invite new comers, prepare the small group lesson, make any other arrangements, and above all, train new leadership to lead the new small groups. It's a total package. If the small group leader only focuses on evangelism, many will slip out the back door. If he only centers his attention on discipleship, the group will grow inward and probably stagnate. If the leader concentrates solely on small group dynamics, leadership development will suffer. Effective small group leaders possess a clear aim for the group and gently lead the group to fulfill the goal of multiplication.[2]

Spiritual Parenting: The Call of Every Believer

The key to successful multiplication is understanding the role of every believer as spiritual parents. People today are starving for relationships. Churches, hopefully unintentionally, have "institutionalized" the process of raising their spiritual children. Believers are encouraged to attend services and get involved in church-wide events, programs or departments, yet there is little emphasis on getting intimately involved in the lives of other believers. The theory is that more involvement and teaching will mature the new believer. Although these activities are important, they will never fill the void of relationships.

Just as a natural child needs the ongoing covering and involvement of a parent in the process of maturing, so does a new believer need a spiritual parent. Unfortunately, many mature believers have filled their schedules with other responsibilities and have turned to the church (the institution) to raise their spiritual children. This problem has existed ever since the birth of the Church. The Apostle Paul writes to the church in Corinth regarding their lack of spiritual parenting. In 1 Corinthians 4:15 he writes,

"For though you might have ten thousand instructors in Christ, yet you do not have many fathers; for in Christ Jesus I have begotten you through the gospel."

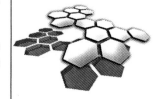

The responsibility of small group leaders is to become spiritual parents to those we are called to lead. It is then through our example that they will also receive the anointing and revelation to parent those they are leading.

Spiritual Parenting is a Process

Jesus modeled the process of spiritual parenting with His disciples. It took a great deal of time and energy to turn twelve raw recruits into world changers. Those that have had children understand that raising children is a process that takes a great deal of time, energy and sacrifice. The process of raising mature, godly, healthy children cannot be accomplished in a matter of weeks. The process can take years!

This logic must be applied to spiritual parenting as well. Our commitment to them should be no different. Unfortunately, many come in looking for relationship to guide and direct them only to feel abandoned, shifted from class to class or teacher to pastor, and never feel as if there is someone who cares about their life. They become spiritual orphans.

Small group leaders should impart this crucial truth into every person in their group, commit to the role of spiritual parents and understand that this process will cost time, energy and sacrifice. Illustrated on the following page is the parallel between natural and spiritual parenting.

The Parenting Process

INFANCY *(0-2 Years Old)*

Early development years. Learning to walk, talk, and eat. Great deal of energy and attention is required during these formative years.

MEMBER *(0-1 Years)*

New people brought to Christ and they begin their spiritual walk learning how to walk with Christ. Character is established, Membership is encouraged.

CHILDHOOD *(2-10 Years Old)*

Critical years where foundation of morals, values, and world view are established. Boundaries are set up, disciplines are developed, and the educational foundation is positioned. The child becomes more confident and dependent on the parent, but much supervision is still required.

POTENTIAL LEADER *(1+ Years)*

Member is encouraged to take next step in the development process. Greater convictions, morals, and values are established. Deeper revelation to God's Word and further training is given to build a sure foundation. Small Group involvement begins to move towards more leadership tasks, while still being groomed by the Small Group Leader.

ADOLESCENT *(11-18 Years Old)*

This is the stage where all the foundations are tested, tried, and purged. Implementation of many earlier principles are engaged. Challenge of rules and authority may exist. Development of their own convictions and opinions. Independence is established. Life goals are being developed.

ASSISTANT LEADER *(1-2+ Years)*

Individual is now asked to take Small Group Leadership Training. Relationships are strengthened, gifts and skills are developed, and leadership principles are learned. Character is refined and tested. More Cell leadership is given and person is being groomed to become a leader.

MARRIAGE/ADULTHOOD
(11-18 Years Old)

Many leave home and are married during this time frame. The testing of their own morals, values, gifts, and talents are now completely engaged. Separation from the parent brings new understanding of responsibilities as an adult. Maturity takes place as adjustments are sure.

SMALL GROUP LEADER *(2+ Years)*

A new Small Group begins and all leadership lessons become reality as they are implemented in real life situations. New phase of relationship with their spiritual parent emerges and a new sense of responsibility and maturity forms. The call to parenting a new group is now their first priority.

BIRTHING *(21+ Years Old)*

New life comes into existence through the birth of a child. The process of parenting begins a new cycle. All of what has been taught and learned from other generations is now imparted to the new children.

BIRTHING *(3+ Years)*

New life comes into existence as the new Small Group Leaders begin to birth their own Leaders and Small Groups. This process is a continual flow. New generations of Leaders are now required to continue the process of spiritual parenting

NATURAL PARENTING

SPIRITUAL PARENTING

Recruiting and Raising Up Future Small Group Leaders

As a church continues to fulfill the mandate of reaching the lost, many new people will be added to the church on a regular basis. With that, the need for small group leaders will continue to increase if we are to parent each person God brings our way. Without new small groups, the needs of the multitudes that have been entrusted to us will overwhelm existing leadership, causing fatigue and, eventually, burnout at every level.

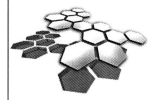

It is important to remember that the continual process of raising up new leaders is our mandate. They are our spiritual children. God desires that *every* person He brings our way has the opportunity to reach their full potential. Much of that responsibility is placed upon the leadership of the church, and not just the individual. Often times we look past those not showing any apparent signs of potential, which minimizes both the Holy Spirit to do His job, as well as our ability to do our job—which is to raise healthy, active, *reproducing* members! Once a small group is infected with the idea that only a few can lead in the group, many will become frustrated, take on a spectator mentality and stagnate in their maturation process. Potentially every person can lead!

We must work to develop every person into reaching their full potential. One of the greatest ways to increase the leadership base in a small group is not to just look to one assistant leader or potential leader to help with all of the small group responsibilities, but to activate *every* person. The purpose of the **Personal Growth Chart**, mentioned in Chapter Five, is to objectively monitor the progress of *every* person and have an *intentional* plan to develop them into becoming spiritual parents themselves. We must commit ourselves 100% to the release and development of God's gifts in all believers.

The Personal Growth Chart

The foundation for multiplying yourself is found in the ongoing mentoring and relational process with those you are raising up. However, there are effective tools that can assist you in being more proactive and intentional in the process. The primary tool used to monitor the progress of this multiplication process is the Personal Growth Chart. Each small group leader will spend time with their leader using this chart once the small group birthing process begins.[3] Please see an example of City Bible Church's chart on the following page for further visual aid. For a blank template, please refer to the Appendix, page 168.

Beginning the Process

Once you have located the Personal Growth Chart you will want to gather the names of all those that are, or will be, attending your small group. The next steps include:

❑ Write the names of every person in your group in the "name" category.

❑ Check off the boxes that apply to attributes already functioning in the people in your small group. Follow the practical steps as outlined later in this chapter.

Stage One: Calling - Church Attendee/Members - Infancy

Once you have the chart filled out with names and existing boxes checked, begin making plans to reproduce yourself and your small group. The goal is to make every person in your small group an active, healthy, reproducing member of the local church. Here are a few points to consider in starting your process of bringing everyone through the "Church Attendee/Members" process.

❑ Begin the process by planning regular meetings with the leaders of your small group. This may include your Assistant(s), Host Home(s), and Potential Leader(s). This meeting could be conducted bi-weekly or monthly.

❑ Components of the regular small group planning meeting should include relationship, prayer, interaction, and planning.

Personal Growth & Development Chart

District # _____

Small Group Leader

Lay Pastor

District Pastor

Name

Infancy / CALLING / Member - M	Salvation / Turning Points
	Water Baptized
	Holy Spirit Baptized
	Attends Weekend services regularly
	Attends Small Groups regularly
	Attends School of Equipping
	Gives Tithes and Offerings
	Enjoys regular personal prayer, Word, and worship
	Heart for winning the lost / City & World
	Upholds family values
	Completed New Members class
	Loves God with heart, soul, mind, and strength
Childhood / TRAINING / Potential Leader - PL	DP/LP approval for Potential Leader
	Good People skills
	Servant attitude
	Emotionally stable
	Strong character
	Performs tasks effectively
	Follows through
	Makes right decisions
	Family / marriage in order
Adolescence / SENDING / Assistant Leader - A	DP/LP approval for Assistant
	Complete Small Group Leader's Training
	Train/Assist discussion times
	Train/Assist planning meeting
	Train/Assist pastoral care
	Train/Assist outreach
	Train/Assist assimilation
	Train/Assist counseling
	Train/Assist administration/reports/forms
	Train/Assist running entire group
	Earned respect and trust of people
Marriage / REPRODUCING / Cell Leader - L	DP/LP approval for new Small Group birth
	Plan type and timing of Group
	Choose team
	Contact Small Group Leader
	Plan date to launch new Group
	Plan Cell "Send Out" meeting
	Contact LP/DP to Attend
	Send out new Small Group team
	Contact frequently

❑ Before planning your small group meeting, take out the chart and identify where each person is in the personal growth process.

❑ Pull out your monthly small group notes or plans and use them along with your Personal Growth Chart in planning all meetings and activities.

❑ Review your plans and delegate various responsibilities to individuals as needed. Delegate to those in leadership attending your meeting as well as to those on your Personal Growth Chart. The level of maturity will determine the degree of responsibility (e.g. leading a discussion vs. bringing a snack).

❑ Spend a few minutes to pray for every person on your Personal Growth Chart and for the areas you would like to see each person grow in.

❑ Once the meeting is finished, contact each person not at the meeting and ask them to assist in the area discussed. These calls could be done by yourself or by one of the people from your planning meeting.

❑ Encourage every person to take additional steps in the personal growth/ multiplication process. The goal as a small group leader is to assist in the maturation process of every believer. This would include any recommended classes, water baptism, etc.

❑ Make sure to monitor the faithfulness to attendance, willingness to be involved, people skills, gifts, and character for a season *before* asking them to become a designated potential leader.

❑ Pray that the Lord would guide you in choosing potential leaders.

❑ Get feedback and counsel from your supervisor before asking anyone to be involved in any leadership tasks.

❑ Observe people as they work with others in the group. Watch those who lead conversations, are leading out in prayer, willing to serve in any capacity, etc.

❑ Talk with them about their relationship with God, with the church and with their family.

❑ Evaluate potential leaders by asking the following questions:
   • Are they spiritually qualified?
   • Do they have good social skills, potential leader skills?
   • Do they embrace the vision of the church and small groups?
   • Are they developing godly character?

Stage Two: Training - Potential Leaders - Childhood
Once you have identified a potential leader, follow the guidelines listed below.

❑ Contact your supervisor and get permission to approach them about becoming a potential leader.

❑ Set up a meeting and discuss your desire to work closely with them. Be sure to encourage them about their potential and how the Lord could use them in the future.

❑ Begin inviting them to your small group planning meetings with your other leaders. Delegate a portion of the meeting and allow them to lead.

❑ Meet regularly to discuss their progress and to deal with areas that may need attention. Don't be afraid to gently adjust and correct. Their ability to receive instruction will be an indication of their desire to be taught.

❑ Make sure you are developing character as well as skills. Listed below is a chart from *Leading Life-Changing Small Groups* by Bill Donahue.[4]

Character	Skills
• Must be developed	• Can be provided
• Takes time	• Takes practice and time
• Can disqualify from leadership	• Can delay leadership
• Is an inward measure	• Are an outward measure
• Tested in adversity, but developed in the quiet	• Practiced in quiet time but tested in adversity
• Involves relationship with God/Others	• Involves relationship to the task

❑ Watch for "negative identification marks" and work with the individual to correct them.
  • Inability to keep confidences
  • Hasty in making decisions
  • Constant poor judgments (even after instructions)
  • Aggressive and domineering in relationships
  • Emotional instability
  • Pushing for promotion and recognition
  • Constantly on the wrong side of decisions
  • Continual conflicts with those under their charge
  • Continual justifying and blame-shifting

❑ Review the qualifications of a small group leader and work to accomplish each qualification with your potential leader.

❑ Encourage them to attend the next small group leaders training course

Stage Three: Sending - Assistants - Adolescence
Once you have walked through the member and potential leader stages, the next phase is to move them into the role of an assistant. It is recommended that you have at least two assistants in your group. This will allow you to have a strong leadership base, as well as the ability to continually birth new small groups.

❑ Make your potential leader an official assistant small group leader. Encourage them to attend leadership meetings at the church.

❑ Take them to your church-wide small group leadership meetings.

❑ Meet with your new assistant and explain the criteria on the Personal Growth Chart in the section labeled, "Assistants." Explain how you will work with them in training during their small group leader's training class.

❑ Allow your new assistant to oversee occasional meetings, and to fill in for you whenever you are away. Spend time after the meeting encouraging

and equipping them for greater success.

❑ Delegate some evangelism or administrative work to your assistant on an ongoing basis.

❑ Follow the method of tracking, monitoring, and modifying leadership development in your new assistant by constant review of the Personal Growth Chart.

❑ Work closely in training the new assistant in conjunction with their small group leader's training class. This will give the new assistant practical application, hands-on learning, and instruction during their leadership development process.

❑ Determine the timing for birthing a new small group. This can be determined by the size of the group, the leadership strength of the group, or other needs in the church. The date should also be at least eight weeks away to give ample time for planning and preparation.[5]

❑ Once a date is determined, contact your supervisor and determine who will work with your assistant as their mentor in the birthing process.

❑ Begin the process. Complete details regarding the development of your small group leaders, host home, location, and people.

❑ Promote the new small group birth (explained later on in this chapter) in your group.

Stage Four: Reproducing - New Small Group Leaders/Marriage - Adulthood
The final stage is to reproduce your small group by birthing a new small group. It has been said, "You never reach true fulfillment in ministry until you have spiritual grandchildren."[6]

❑ Discuss what method will be used in birthing a new small group. There are nine different options, which are explained later in this chapter.

❑ Confirm those who will be leaving to begin the new small group birth.

❑ Contact each person to discuss the move and encourage their support.

❑ Plan a special "Small Group Birthing Party" with your existing group. Make it a joyful group celebration, invite other church leadership, and spend some time praying over the new leader. Allow other group members to share their positive thoughts and feelings about the leader being sent out.

❑ Once you have birthed the new group, keep in contact with the leader and continue to encourage them on their new venture. Communicate with your supervisor regarding any observations or insight you may have.

❑ Plan an occasional meeting to combine the groups for a special celebration.

❑ Begin working with your other potential leaders and assistants, and set a goal for your next small group birthing date.

Birthing New Small Groups

There are many ways in which a small group can be birthed. Each small group has its own special set of circumstances that make it impossible to follow any one method of birthing for the entire church. Different seasons in your group may dictate one type of birthing instead of a previously-used method. The gifting and vision of the new group leader may also determine the type of group being launched.

The actual method adopted for each new group must be carefully planned and reviewed. Your small group leadership should work closely with each group leader in planning what method best fits each situation. The following pages give nine examples of how you might birth new small groups from your existing

Option #1

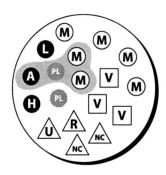

Assistant Small Group Leader births a new small group with a Potential Leader and a few members of the group at a new location.

Option #2

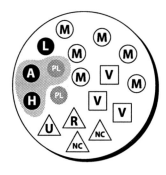

Assistant Small Group Leader births a new small group with the existing host home and a Potential Leader. Small Group Leader and remaining group find a new host home.

Option #3

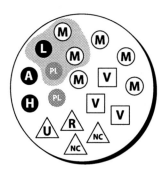

Small Group Leader births a new small group with a Potential Leader and a few members of the group at a new location. The Assistant Small Group Leader takes over the existing group in the existing Host Home.

Option #4

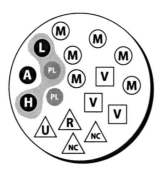

Small Group Leader births a new small group with the Host Home and a Potential Leader. The Assistant Small Group Leader takes over the existing group and finds a new location.

Option #5

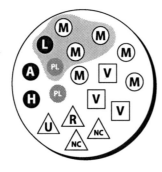

Small Group splits. Small Group Leader and Assistant split the group and one group finds a new Host Home.

Option #6

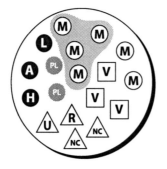

Part of an existing small group moves to a small group that is smaller to balance group size and ad growth and stability to struggling cells.

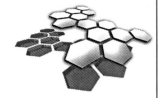

Option #7

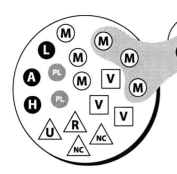

Part of an existing group moves to a new small group with a transplanted new Leader and Assistant to begin a new small group.

Option #8

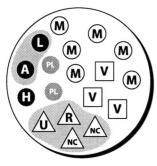

Create a sub-Small Group consisting of a Small Group Leader or an Assistant with a new convert or rededication and their unsaved friends gathering at a separate time than the existing Small Group. This creates an opportunity to penetrate relational sphere of New Converts.

Option #9

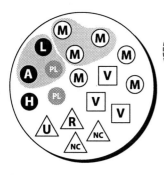

Create a sub-Small Group, focusing primarily on evangelism. Primary is to create outreach group of existing Small Group to reach unsaved contacts of the entire group. As people give their lives to Christ, they can be added to the existing Small Group or a new Group could be created.

[1] You can order *The Covenants* class on tape through Church Leadership Training Institute, a ministry of City Bible Church by calling 503-255-3540 or by email at clti@pbccollege.org.

[2] Joel Comiskey, *Leadership Explosion*, Touch Publications, copyright 2000, p. 40.

[3] City Bible Church uses the *Small Group Coaching Guide,* which is a tool that assists new small group leaders in the successful planning and birthing of a new small group. To order a copy call City Christian Publishing at 800-777-6057.

[4] Bill Donahue, *Leading Life-Changing Small Groups*, Zondervan Publishing House, 1996, p.70.

[5] For an example of how this process is conducted at City Bible Church, see the *Small Group Coaching Guide* which is a tool that assist new small group Leaders in the successful planning and birthing of a new group. To order a copy call City Christian Publishing at 800-777-6057.

[6] Quote by Shawn Kearney, minister from Australia.

INTERCESSION AND THE SMALL GROUP

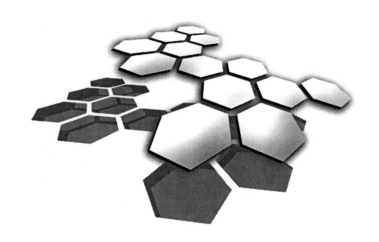

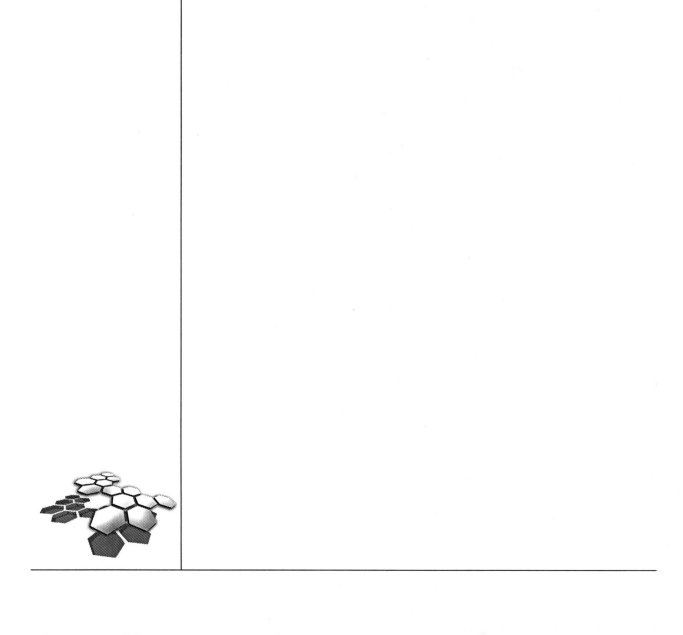

Intercession and the Small Group
Chapter Seven

The world is experiencing a global prayer awakening. The spirit of prayer is sweeping every country of the world that has a hunger and openness to the Holy Spirit. We venture into new territory as we seek to understand the potent ministry of prayer-intercession. This is vital to our future and essential to fulfilling our vision.

The key ingredient to accomplishing these outreaching goals is intercessory prayer. This is a high calling with a price to pay, but the benefits far outweigh the costs. Small group leaders should be on the frontline of grasping and embracing the ministry of intercession and be determined to turn themselves and their group into a people zealous to see the fulfillment of God's purposes. Our goal is to raise up interceding small groups one person at a time.

Seven Basic Truths Regarding Intercession

1. Intercessory prayer is found in Scripture from Genesis to Revelation as a definite kind of prayer God responds to.

2. Intercessory prayer is modeled by many of God's chosen vessels who practiced the ministry of intercession with awesome results.

3. Intercessory prayer was a prayer commitment of the first apostles, the first disciples, and the first church.

4. Intercessory prayer was, and is, the chief ministry of our Lord Jesus Christ, who is the mediator between God and man and is now the Intercessor for man.

5. Intercessory prayer is the responsibility of every church that is ruled by Christ and His Word.

6. Intercessory prayer is being restored to the Church world-wide in what might be the greatest unified emphasis since the first church in the book of Acts.

7. Intercessory prayer is a call of the Spirit to our churches today for the taking of our neighborhoods, cities, regions, and nations for the Kingdom of God.[1]

The Importance of Prayer and Intercession

Prayer and intercession are important for every Christian. As a small group leader, it is critical to model and impart to your entire small group the necessity for prayer and intercession in each of their daily lives. Here are twelve reasons why every Christian should have a vibrant, healthy prayer-intercession ministry. These twelve principles have been taken from the book, *Seasons of Intercession* by Pastor Frank Damazio, and is available through City Christian Publishing. This is recommended reading for every believer.[2]

1. Christ left us an example of the importance of prayer (see Matthew 14:23; Mark 1:35; Luke 6:12; 3:21, 5:16, 9:18).

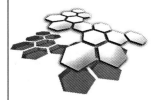

2. The Apostles left us an example of the importance of prayer (see Acts 1: 14, 4:31, 6:4, 12:5, 13:3, 16:3, 21:5).

3. Prayer is God's method for obtaining joy (see John 16:24; Acts 16:25).

4. Prayer keeps us spiritually fit and alert (see Matthew 26:41; Luke 21:34-36; 1 Peter 4:7; Jude 20).

5. Prayer enables us to receive wisdom and the mind of God (see James 1: 5; Acts 1:24, 10:9, 13:3, 14:23; Luke 6:12-13).

6. Prayer transforms us into the image of Christ (see Luke 9:28-29).

7. Prayer is God's means of obtaining our material and spiritual desires (see Matthew 7:7-8; John 14:13-14, 15:7, 16:23-24).

8. Prayer moves the hand of God to work in the affairs of men (see Exodus 3:7, 14:10-11, 10:15; Jonah 2:1; Acts 12:5; James 5:17).

9. Prayer expresses our dependence upon God (see John 15:5; Zechariah 4:6).

10. Through prayer we gain freedom from worry (see Philippians 4:6-7; Psalm 22:1-5).

11. Prayer unleashes the power and blessing of God (see 2 Chronicles 6-7; Acts 1-2, 4:23-31).

12. Prayer teaches us to know Christ intimately (see Jude 20-21; Philippians 3:10; Colossians 1:9).

Intercession is for Every Believer

The ministry of intercession has been given to every believer in the Body of Christ. The gift of intercessory prayer is not a gift found in just a few believers in the church, it is a gift given to the entire church as a whole. There are those who carry a deeper burden for intercessory prayer than others, but this does not mean that the gift of intercession resides in some members, and not others. All churches are to be interceding churches.

Every small group leader, assistant, and attender must move forward and take this responsibility as their own. They must say and believe, "I am called to intercession!"

Intercession is the Key to a Successful Small Group and a Healthy Church

Many years ago, the main means of transporting people and cargo across vast regions of the country was by steam engine trains. For miles, you could hear the sound of the steam blowing and engines roaring as these beautiful machines chugged towards their destination. They were huge, explosive, and awesome, and there was nothing that could slow them down. A closer look at these incredible machines shows that there was a small compartment in the main engine car where the engineer would throw coal. This hotbed of explosive flames produced the power and steam necessary to move these massive trains forward.

The church is one of the most beautiful pieces of machinery ever created by God. It is the instrument God uses to move His stated purposes forward. He also has created a small compartment that is at the center of the church which produces the power and steam necessary for moving the Church forward towards her final destination. This hotbed of fiery coals is called intercessory prayer.[3]

Perhaps there is no other ingredient as important as intercessory prayer. It must become the foundation to everything that is done in the small group. There are seven Greek words for prayer in the New Testament. Four of those are used in the following verse given by the Apostle Paul to the church in Ephesus:

Ephesians 6:18 "Praying always with all prayer and supplication in the Spirit, being watchful to this end with all perseverance and supplication for all the saints."

Developing Intercessory Coverage for Yourself and the Small Group

As we move ahead in fulfilling the vision God has placed before us, intercession is not only the fire that launches us forward, but the protective agent which keeps us from the attack of the enemy. We must not be ignorant of the enemy's tactics, but move forward soberly and vigilantly, relying on intercession as our primary shield.

1 Peter 5:8 "Be sober, be vigilant; because your adversary the devil walks about like a roaring lion, seeking whom he may devour."

1 Timothy 2:1 "Therefore I exhort first of all that supplications, prayers, intercessions, and giving of thanks be made for all men,"

At every level of leadership in the local church, you should find one common thread—intercession for every leader and every department. The thread of intercession should be woven throughout the small group as well. Every small group leader must be involved in intercession. The following section gives some suggestions for implementing intercession into your life, your family and your group. These principles have been taken from the procedures developed by Mark Jones, Prayer Pastor at City Bible Church, and modified to fit small group ministry.

1. Come to the awareness of your need to receive personal prayer coverage. Acknowledge that intercession will make a critical difference in the success and protection of your small group ministry.

2. Ask God to reveal a few people who would commit to praying for you and the small group. These individuals may include your assistant, potential leaders, host, or members in the group. Although these individuals may make the best group to pray for you, do not eliminate the possibility of others outside the group, with whom you have close relationships.

3. Choose those with whom you have an existing relationship and are confident of their character. You want to find those whom you can trust with intimate details of your life. Confidentiality is a key ingredient to the ongoing success of your team.

4. Begin to pray for God to show you those who you may link with in praying for you and your group.

5. Contact those you desire to pray with and invite them to participate in interceding together.

6. Bring the group together for an initial meeting and share your vision for praying for each other and for the group.

7. Get together at least once a month. You may want to plan to get together right before every small group meeting. Allow enough time for concentrated prayer and soaking times in His presence. You may also want to send them a weekly update via email.

8. Grow with your intercessory partners. Let the trust you develop dictate the "width and depth" to which you open up with them.

9. Don't hesitate to alert your prayer partners of urgent situations that might develop between regular times of contact.

10. Don't neglect to keep your Intercessory Team active and in force! The enemy does not want anyone to succeed in developing intercessory prayer coverage. Press forward to see the team established, maintained, and moving forward.

11. Intercessory partners are not to replace your personal prayer life. They are an addition to it. Each person will "stand in the gap," "build hedges" and "bind and loose" on your behalf. Be consistent in wearing your full armor daily. Nothing is to replace your personal time and relationship with the Lord.

Opening Your Small Group in Intercession

Jesus said, *"My house shall be a house of prayer* (see Matthew 21:13).*"* This principle is embraced at corporate gatherings and should also be included in the small group meeting. People need to see the importance of prayer not only taught, but implemented on every level. Prayer does make a difference!

Here are a few tips for opening your small group with prayer (Please keep in mind this may not apply to every meeting. The focus and purpose of each meeting may vary. Please use as it applies).

1. Be sensitive to first-time visitors. Explain that every meeting begins with prayer and that prayer is "simply talking to God." Encourage every person to participate.

2. Direct the people in a time of corporate prayer together. This prayer should be to get every person to focus on God, get rid of any distractions or sins, and prepare their heart to receive from God during the small group meeting.

3. Give an opportunity for the group to break up into twos and threes and minister to each other.

4. Bring the group back together by ending in a corporate prayer or a song.

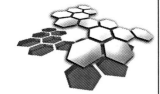

How to Pray for People in Your Small Group

Every person and church has its own unique style of prayer. The methods you use may be slightly different than others around you. As you carefully move forward in praying for people in your group, here are a few tips that may help enhance the effectiveness and fruitfulness of your prayers.

1. Pray for those who appear to want prayer. You will find those who are expressing an openness to the Holy Spirit are more receptive to prayer than those who may seem distracted.

2. Work with the Holy Spirit. Observing the person's response to the Holy Spirit can assist you in cooperating with what God is doing in the person's heart.

3. Take time to minister to people. Don't rush the prayer time. Allowing people to be bathed in prayer will increase the effectiveness of the prayer ministry.

4. Be sensitive to those who are being ministered to by the Holy Spirit. Try and keep others from distracting or bumping the individual.

5. Do not minister to someone who doesn't want to be prayed for or doesn't ask for ministry. Allow God to work in their hearts and draw them to Himself in His time.

6. Use discretion. Under the influence of the Holy Spirit, people will often reveal issues of a very personal nature. As small group leaders, we must hold these secrets confidentially.

7. Pray quietly with people about sensitive matters.

What to Pray in a Small Group

Here are some suggestions on how to get started praying for individuals in your small group.

1. Respond to the need. When you ask if there are individuals needing prayer, be sure to be ready to take time and minister to the individual. Be sensitive to the time, but don't cut off the moving of the Holy Spirit.

2. Use the Bible as a guide for prayer. Using scriptural promises and principles as tools of intercession gives you the freedom to minister effectively while remaining safe.

3. Always pray positive prayers. We are to comfort, encourage and exhort with love. Never pray demeaning, judgmental or critical prayers in any form.

4. Receive direction from the Holy Spirit. The Bible says in Romans 8:14, *"Those that are led by the Spirit of God, these are the sons of God."* Be spirit-led in the prayer times and ask the Holy Spirit to reveal the words to pray.

5. Don't give personal prophecy. We are to encourage and pray for God's will to be done in people's lives, but not give direct prophecy that may derail their lives. If you feel a strong word for any individual, talk with your Lay Pastor before sharing anything specific.

6. Frame impressions and intuitions into fact-finding questions. If you feel impressed to pray a certain way, you may ask, "Does this mean anything to you?" If their answer is yes, you then have a platform from which to pray, instead of a "Thus says God" prayer that could turn into a disaster.

[1] Frank Damazio, *Seasons of Intercession,* City Christian Publishing, 1998, p. 18.

[2] Ibid, p. 78.

[3] Analogy from Dr. Mark Jones, Prayer Pastor at City Bible Church.

PASTORAL CARE
IN THE
SMALL GROUP

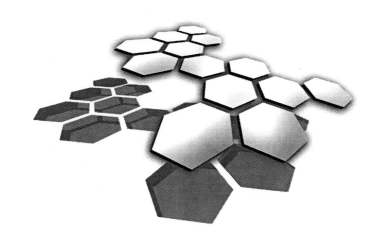

Pastoral Care in the Small Group
Chapter Eight

As mentioned in earlier chapters, the role of a small group leader is a shepherding role. The most effective and personal way to pastor any congregation is at its smallest denominator, the small group. The relationships established in a small group can be as fruitful and effective as relationships established with staff pastors. People relate best to those with whom they have established an existing, personal, intimate relationship.

Being a shepherd over others is an awesome responsibility. Groups should be purposefully designed to remain small so that every person receives quality pastoral care without overwhelming the leader. This chapter will give you assistance in successfully pastoring those in your small group.

Insights from the Net

The word net is defined as "an open-meshed fabric twisted, knotted, or woven together at regular intervals."[1] The strength of the net depends on the number of twists or knots made. The net must be pulled and stretched into place.

The word *network* is defined as, "a network that is held together by secure connections; a network is the total sum of its parts."[2]

The Bible gives a clear understanding of how Christians are to build relational nets to strengthen the body of Christ. The greater the number of relationships, the stronger the net.

1. Knit Together (see Ephesians 4:16; Colossians 2:2)

2. Joined Together (see 1 Corinthians 1:10; Ephesians 2:21)

3. Built Together (see Ephesians 2:2)

4. Many Members (see 1 Corinthians 12:26)

5. One Body (see 1 Corinthians 12:12-14)

6. Every Joint Supplies (see Ephesians 4:16)

The parallel between building strong nets and building strong small groups is obvious. Each small group should be a network of believers that are held together by secure relationships and inter-dependency on one another. A small group is only as strong as its weakest relationship.

The Pastoral Process: Everything Begins With the Small Group

The traditional approach to pastoring directs all needs and decisions to the staff pastoral team. In smaller churches the Senior Pastor usually takes on all of the responsibilities of marrying, burying, preaching, counseling, teaching, and leading. Whenever the pastor comes to the level where he can no longer meet the needs

of all the people, the church stops growing because the needs exceed his ability to manage them. Even in larger churches, paid pastoral staff are hired to "pastor the people." However, just like the pastor of the smaller church, he too has a limit he can handle. Whenever the church grows to a point where it can afford another pastor, one is hired to then take care of the additional needs.

The Bible has a different plan regarding the pastoral process. From the time of Moses being reprimanded by his father-in-law Jethro in Exodus 18, through to Paul's challenge to the Ephesians in Chapter 4, the call has been to *"equip the saints for the work of ministry."* This approach inverts traditional methods and places the responsibility on mobilized members of a congregation to pastor, and for the full-time pastor to equip the believers to fulfill their mandate.

This biblical approach is the only way the church can fulfill the mission of reaching all nations. The responsibilities are too great for the five-fold ministry to handle by themselves. When a church can truly equip its people to become the pastoral arm for the harvest, the possibilities are limitless.

This does not mean that the small group leader is the only person who deals with the pastoral challenges. Other church leadership will be working closely with the small group leaders to assist in any situation that needs additional help.

Pastoring in the Small Group

One of the clearest scriptures concerning the shepherd's responsibility to his flock is found in Ezekiel 34. God rebukes Israel's shepherds for not giving proper pastoral care to their flock. It is evident that they were to be feeders, leaders, gatherers, and builders of the people.

The Bible uses the relationship of a shepherd to his sheep as a comparison of how leaders are to relate and care for their people. Sheep need a shepherd, and God's people need pastoral care and oversight. A small group leader is assuming the position and responsibility of a True Shepherd. Let's review a biblical perspective of people with and without the shepherding principle.

Sheep / People with a True Shepherd

1. Sheep receive provision (see Psalms 23:1-2).

2. Sheep receive direction (see Numbers 27:15-17; Psalms 80:1).

3. Sheep are fruitful (see Jeremiah 23:3).

4. Sheep are kept (see Jeremiah 31:10).

5. Sheep are strengthened (see Ezekiel 34:4,16).

6. Sheep are fed (see Jeremiah 23:4; 1 Peter 5:2).

7. Sheep receive healing (see Ezekiel 34:4,16).

8. Sheep receive binding up (see Ezekiel 34:4,16).

9. Sheep are found (see Ezekiel 34:15; John 10:16).

10. Sheep are safe (see Ezekiel 34:25).

11. Sheep receive rest (see Psalms 23:2; Ezekiel 34:15).

12. Sheep are comforted (see Psalms 23:4).

13. Sheep are restored (see Psalms 23:3).

14. Sheep are visited (see Jeremiah 23:2).

15. Sheep receive increase (see Jeremiah 23:3).

Sheep / People without a True Shepherd

1. Sheep are scattered (see Zechariah 13:7; Ezekiel 34:5-6).

2. Sheep wander (see Ezekiel 34:6).

3. Sheep are lacking (see Jeremiah 23:4).

4. Sheep are devoured (see Ezekiel 34:5).

5. Sheep are weak (see Matthew 9:36).

6. Sheep have needs (see Psalms 23:1).

7. Sheep are diseased (see Ezekiel 34:4).

8. Sheep are broken (see Ezekiel 34:4).

9. Sheep are lost (see Ezekiel 34:4).

10. Sheep are prey for the enemy (see Ezekiel 34:8).

11. Sheep are fearful (see Jeremiah 23:4; Psalms 23:4).

12. Sheep are despondent (see Jeremiah 23:3).

13. Sheep are destroyed (see John 10:10).

14. Sheep are divided (see Acts 20:30).

15. Sheep are robbed (see John 10:1-2).

There is an important principle found in these two categories that deserves attention. This is the concept of "proactive pastoring." In the first category it is evident which qualities of the sheep are the desired result. Furthermore, these attributes are best developed in the lives of younger Christians through leaders that take the time and energy to initiate the process of spiritual growth and maturity. Indeed, all people are responsible for their own destiny, but we as leaders must take a proactive approach to mentoring those entrusted to our care.

The second category is the least desired type of sheep. Unfortunately many Christians fall into this category. Could it be that our "reactive" approach to pastoring has contributed to their unhealthy condition? Pastoring is much more than waiting

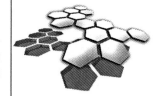

for the phone to ring to deal with the next crisis or counseling situation. With these thoughts in mind, let's discuss a CARE strategy for every person attending your church.

Caring in the Small Group

In Acts 2:44-45 we see evidence of a community of believers that truly cared for one another. This is the biblical model we are to follow. "All the believers were together and had everything in common. Selling their possessions and goods, they gave to anyone as he had need."

One of the primary purposes of the small group is to be a "caring unit." Once relationships are formed, the process of identifying and meeting needs is a very natural process. By nature, people want to take care of the needs of those whom they love. The more mature the small group becomes in their relationships, the more willing people are to come together to meet the needs of those in crisis. In addition, if there is a "harvesting mindset" the group will also have the desire to minister to the new people God is bringing in to their small group as well.

It is our goal as leaders to provide all leadership with the tools necessary to effectively pastor every person God sends our way. The following pages will explain the procedures available to the small group leaders of the church.

Caring through _____.
Each small group should be involved in assisting the people in their group at special times and seasons. The leader will take care of the situation but will also notify their supervisor as to what is taking place. If necessary, other leadership may be contacted or involved in the process.

❑ _____

❑ _____

❑ _____

❑ _____

❑ _____

❑ _____

❑ _____

Caring for _____.
Every small group, some time or later, will be involved with people in financial need. The following criteria explains our church policy regarding financial assistance:

❑   Designated funds are given to the following situations:

❑   Designated funds will not be given to cases such as:

❑   Procedure for obtaining financial assistance through the church:

Caring for Needs _____ .
Any crisis that arises should be confronted with intercessory prayer. With this conviction as a major distinctive of the church, we have developed specific prayer strategies that will engage prayer for needs within the small group.

Any need, large or small, should be covered in prayer. As mentioned in a previous chapter, "Intercession in the Small Group," there are a variety of ways to communicate prayer needs, as discussed below.

❑ Our Church Crisis Prayer Plan

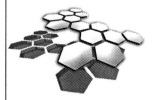

Conflict in the Small Group

There is one unfortunate component that may surface in your small group. A by-product of building relationships is conflict, which is a part of the development process. Without proper conflict management, your small group could experience disagreements, discord and division. The first step toward dealing with conflict is to understand how it is caused.

Causes of Conflict among the _____.

1. When there is a misunderstanding during the group meeting between two individuals who have a difference of opinion.

2. When someone corrects or disciplines another person's child.

3. When slanderous or stabbing comments are made toward someone else in the group either in private or in front of others.

4. When someone does not follow through on an obligation they have promised to fulfill.

5. When a child disrupts the meeting or destroys something in another's home.

6. When someone holds or hides resentment that comes from an offense.

7. When someone lives a lifestyle different than the lifestyle of another.

Causes of Conflict from the _____.

1. When there is inconsistency in practicing clear, established biblical principles.

2. When a leader violates moral and ethical standards taught to the people.

3. When the leadership presumptuously declares a vision or direction from the Lord and then abruptly abandons or changes from that direction.

4. When the leadership avoids, procrastinates, or ignores the necessity of confronting and handling the problem of people sowing seeds of contention.

5. When the leadership causes confusion by choosing unqualified leaders to serve the people, thereby violating clearly defined standards and wisdom.

6. When the leadership carelessly handles an explosive situation without considering the ramifications, or makes a hasty decision without prayer.

7. When the leadership does not consistently practice principles of forgiveness (taught in Matthew 18) and thus allows offenses to grow in the church and in the leaders.

8. When the one in leadership acts independently, violating the spirit of team ministry.

Correcting Conflicts with _____.
Our best method of handling conflict is to go to the Word of God as our guide. Below are twelve sure principles to assist in any conflict.

Principle 1: Speak truthfully with love (see Ephesians 4:15,25).

Principle 2: Build up; don't tear down (see Ephesians 4:29-32).

Principle 3: Be as gracious as possible (see Ephesians 4:29-32).

Principle 4: Express honest feelings (see Ephesians 4:26-27).

Principle 5: Don't act in anger (see Ephesians 4:26-27).

Principle 6: Don't involve others in the dispute (see Matthew 18:15-17).

Principle 7: Once dealt with, wipe the slate (see 1 Corinthians 13:5).

Principle 8: Listen more, think before speaking (see Proverbs 15:23,28).

Principle 9: Keep others' interests in mind (see Philippians 2:4).

Principle 10: Don't retaliate (see 1 Peter 3:8-9).

Principle 11: Monitor your own motives (see Proverbs 13:10).

Principle 12: Stay away from vain arguments (see Proverbs 20:3).

Baptism of the Holy Spirit in the Small Group

Next to receiving Jesus Christ as your personal Lord and Savior, one of the most important ingredients in a believer's life is the Baptism of the Holy Spirit. Jesus Himself fulfilled every step only through the ministry and power of the Holy Spirit. His public ministry can be seen in the following powerful scripture.

> *Acts 10:38 "...God anointed Jesus of Nazareth with the Holy Spirit and with power, who went about doing good and healing all who were oppressed by the devil, for God was with Him."*

It is the Lord's intention that we would follow in His steps accomplishing all that He did and more. It is impossible for any Christian to penetrate the darkness and reach a dying world in their own strength. His people are meant to have anointing and power as they minister to other believers and the lost.

In the book, *Preparing to Receive the Baptism of the Holy Spirit,* Richard Heckman states the following truths found in scripture.[3]

1. Jesus said that He could do nothing supernatural apart from the power and presence of the Holy Spirit.

2. Jesus commanded all His followers to receive the Baptism of the Holy Spirit.

3. Receiving the Baptism of the Holy Spirit is a definite experience separate from salvation and water baptism.

4. Like salvation, the Baptism of the Holy Spirit is a free gift from God and is available to every Christian. You will definitely know when you have received this gift.

5. The Baptism of the Holy Spirit is received through faith in God's Word and by believing that it is God's gift for His people today.

Benefits of the Baptism of the Holy Spirit

We are assured great benefits once we have received the Baptism of the Holy Spirit.

1. The Holy Spirit will empower the Church to be witnesses for Him (see Acts 1:8, 2:13, 4:13, 5:28).

2. The Holy Spirit will guide His people into all truth (see John 16:12-13).

3. The Holy Spirit will give us heavenly communication with the Father (see Mark 16:17; 1 Corinthians 14:2-4; Jude 20).

4. The Holy Spirit will increase Godly character in the lives of His followers (see Galatians 5:22-23).

5. The Holy Spirit will give each person their "prayer language" of speaking in tongues, which is the initial evidence of the Baptism of the Holy Spirit (see Acts 2:33; Mark 16:17).

6. The Holy Spirit will teach us to pray (see Luke 11:9,13; Romans 8:26).

7. The Holy Spirit will strengthen us and build us up (see Jude 20; 1 Corinthians 14:4).

8. The Holy Spirit will refresh us in times of need (see Isaiah 28:11-12).

9. The Holy Spirit will assist us in successful spiritual warfare (see Ephesians 6:18).

Leading Others to Receive the Baptism of the Holy Spirit

The Baptism of the Holy Spirit may very well be one of the most significant times in the life of a Christian. This life-changing encounter should never be taken lightly. As a small group leader, your preparation and response to these special times has a great bearing on the outcome of the prayer time with the group or individual with whom you are praying.

Our desire is that every person in our church be baptized in the Holy Spirit. The process of leading people in the Baptism of the Holy Spirit should be continual, as you will always have new people added to your small group. Make sure to make this as a frequent part of your meetings throughout the year. Here are a few tips in helping you with this important task.

1. Make sure to provide an environment free from distractions. If you allow the children to be a part of the main meeting on a regular basis, you may want to separate the younger ones for this part of the meeting.

2. Plan a time where you can minister to people for an extended period of time.

3. Don't rush this special time. You may want to begin the time with prayer and/or worship.

4. Begin praying with those wanting to receive the Baptism of the Holy Spirit by giving an opportunity to remove any sin or uncleanness from their heart.

5. Spend a few minutes praying for the individual and allow the Holy Spirit to come and begin to saturate the individual with His presence. When you sense the right time, begin praying specifically for the Holy Spirit to come and baptize them. An example of this prayer may be, "Father, in the name of Jesus Christ, I pray that You would come and baptize them in Your Holy Spirit. We receive You, and Your power in our lives…"

6. You may need to communicate to the individual to close their eyes, relax and remove other thoughts; minimize the mind and just allow the Holy Spirit to begin to flood their mouth with new language. They may need to be told to open their mouth and cooperate with the Holy Spirit. If their mouth remains shut, it is difficult to speak forth their new tongue.

7. Scripture tells us that speaking in tongues is the initial evidence that someone is baptized in the Holy Spirit. Continue to pray until the person begins to speak in tongues.

8. They should not copy you or someone else that is speaking in tongues. Everyone's prayer language is unique. Some may just receive a few syllables the first time.

9. The Baptism of the Holy Spirit cannot be measured by what they feel. Some feel something, while others do not. We walk by faith, not by feelings.

10. Once the person receives the Baptism of the Holy Spirit, encourage them to continue to speak in tongues for a while and enjoy this fresh new touch of the Spirit in their lives.

11. Encourage each person to use their new prayer language every day.

12. Occasionally there are those who are prayed for that do not receive the Baptism of the Holy Spirit. Often these people can become discouraged or feel that God doesn't care about them. Encourage them that many people have experienced the same situation and remind them that the Lord visited them at a different time. Pray for them and encourage them to be hungry for this gift and to continue to pray to be baptized in the Holy Spirit.

Mobilizing Others in the Small Group

Each person has been given specific gifts and talents to be used in building the Kingdom of God. We are all one body, with one purpose, each providing a certain portion of the greater vision through the use and service of our spiritual gifts.

1 Corinthians 12:12 "For as the body is one and has many members, but all the members of that one body, being many, are one body, so also is Christ."

Romans 12:4-6 "For as we have many members in one body, but all the members do not have the same function, so we, being many, are one body

in Christ, and individually members of one another. Having then gifts differing according to the grace that is given to us, let us use them."

Approximately eighty-five percent of all people who drop out of a church have never "dropped in!" One of the main reasons for attending for only a short time and then leaving is they don't feel they fit in or that they are needed. With that in mind, we need to be working to encourage people to function in different areas of ministry within small groups.

A common mistake made by many leaders is placing people into areas of service based only upon the needs of the group and not the gifting and talents of the individual. There is a place for people to serve and prove themselves as servants, but our first goal should be to place people in areas they will enjoy and grow in.

Although there may not be an abundance of ministry opportunities in a small group, there still are many ways that people can assist in making your small group a success. Here are a few options to consider before asking people to get more involved in a ministry opportunity in your group.

Spiritual Gifts
Spiritual Gifts are supernatural gifts given to man by God. These gifts become tools used by individuals to carry out the purposes of God.

Passion
Placed within each Christian is a specific passion given for the building up of the body of Christ. To some, it may be children's ministry; to others evangelism. God gives each person a certain part of His heart to carry. This is what makes up the body of Christ. Try to determine where a person's burden lies and place them accordingly.

Character and Personality
Some may have a certain gifting and passion, but lack the character to administer the gifts. The gifts of the Spirit are greatly diminished if people lack character in ministering in their areas of gifting. We recommend placing people in areas of service before areas of leadership, so that their character may be tested and proved.

Spiritual Maturity
The length of a person's walk with Christ may not always determine their spiritual maturity level. Some may serve Christ for decades and still be spiritual babes. Spiritual maturity doesn't come by the mere fact that someone prayed a prayer years ago, but by how they have walked out their commitment and allowed the Holy Spirit to transform them into the image of Christ. (see Hebrews 5:12-14)

Natural Talents and Abilities
Each person is born with innate abilities and talents. Some may be naturally gifted in administration, while others may do well in music. In many cases, a person's natural abilities will line up with their spiritual gifts and burdens. That is the beauty of how god created each of us.

Commitment
There may be those in the group that meet every requirement and have all the gifting, talent, and character. Yet if they don't have the time or desire to serve, it is fruitless. Jesus made this clear in the parable of the talents. Some invest,

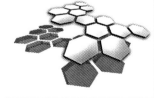

while others bury (see Matthew 25:14-28). Commitment is a key factor. Faithfulness to serve effectively will be a component that you as a leader must look for. In asking people to serve, make sure they understand how much time is involved each week and the length of commitment you are asking from them.

Life Experience
Each group member has a unique set of life experiences that will influence their interests and desires to be active in the group. Group members should be encouraged to allow God to use their life experiences to minister to others in the group.

Availability
Even with the greatest spiritual gifts, passion, character, maturity, talents, abilities, commitment and life experiences, each group member must be able and willing to make time available to the group and its members. Work schedule, family commitments, and life priorities affect availability. The challenge for the small group leader is to help people understand the eternal value of setting aside time to minister to others.

---

[1] *Webster's Ninth New Collegiate Dictionary*, Merriam-Webster Inc. Publishers, 1985 p. 794

[2] Ibid.

[3] Pastor Richard Heckman, *Preparing to Receive the Baptism of the Holy Spirit*, Paraclete Press, 1995.

COUNSELING IN THE SMALL GROUP

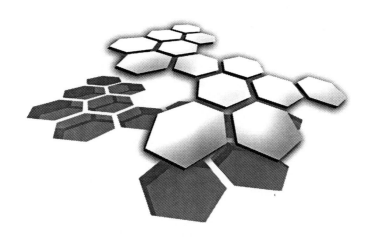

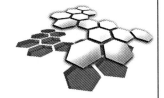

Counseling in the Small Group
Chapter Nine

Almost ninety percent of all counseling situations can be defined as "common care counseling" which can be handled at the small group leader level. Most of these cases can be handled by using common sense, biblical direction, prayer, and a generous portion of care. This section is not designed to give an abundance of counseling techniques, but to give some general guidelines regarding situations you may face. In more severe cases, other church leadership will be available to assist you with the situation.[1]

It is important that all leadership of any local church embrace the same counseling philosophy. Following is a statement that describes the biblical view toward counseling in the local church.

> Counseling is an expression of our pastoral ministry to assist people to become better Christians. Our goal is to aid individuals in understanding and applying the atonement of Christ to their entire lives: past, present and future. We aspire to see Christ's compassion, wisdom and healing power demonstrated. Our frame of reference for counseling is the Bible, which is relevant to all of life's issues. We believe in the sufficiency of the application of Scripture, the dynamics of the Holy Spirit and the ministry of the church in seeing people's deepest needs met. Our counseling ministry will be most effective to those who take personal responsibility and allow the working of both the Word and Spirit in their lives.[1]

As each leader works to provide pastoral care and bring health and restoration to each individual who needs any form of counseling, an understanding of the pastoral care process will assist in meeting a person's needs in a prompt and efficient manner. The following diagrams show the shift in the counseling structure, which allows most people to be ministered to by their small group leaders. The challenges of the old counseling structure and the benefits of the new process are listed for your review. This is a generic diagram of a local church with a small-group pastoring structure.

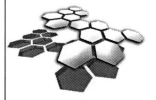

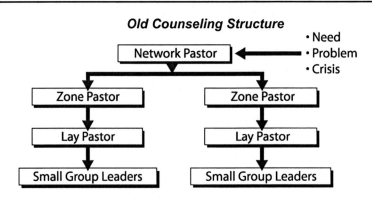

Couseling Challenge

Network Pastor viewed as the main pastor/shepherd.

Needs always directed toward the Network Pastor.

Most needs solved by Network Pastor.

Results in burnout of the Network Pastor.

Results in needs not being met.

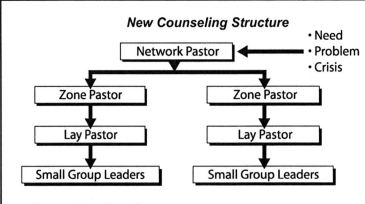

Counseling Benefits

Most needs are common care issues.

Network Pastor viewed as an equipper/shepherd.

Needs directed at all levels.

Most needs begin with the Small Group Leader.

More needs are met at the embroyonic level.

Next level of care is always available.

Church can grow exponentially.

Lay Counselors for specialized or long term care.

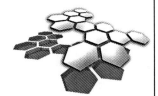

The Pastoral Care/Counseling Process

In order to meet the variety of needs and bring resolution to each challenge presented, there must be very clear goals, plans, and processes established. (See the Appendix page 170 for a sample Pastoral Care Flow Chart.)

Our church has developed the following counseling process:

Policies and Procedures

The following policies are designed to protect all parties involved: the church, the counselor and the counselee. Although these policies may appear to be rigid and strict, they are in place to allow for maximum protection, which in turn provides the platform for effective counseling ministry. Questions or concerns regarding policies and procedures should be directed to your supervisors. The remaining section of this chapter has been taken from the Basic Counseling 101 course, written by Ken and Glenda Malmin, Executive Pastors at City Bible Church and Deans of Portland Bible College.

Each person involved in any form of counseling is to conscientiously follow these policies and procedures.

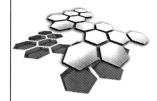

General Counseling Policies and Procedures

1. Each leader is to read and abide by all guidelines set forth in the sections entitled "Policies and Procedures," and "Legal Guidelines."

2. Never make claims of providing "secular counseling."

3. Never make claims that you are a psychotherapist, professional, medical, or psychiatric counselor.

4. Do not use state-regulated professional titles such as, "Licensed Professional Counselor," "Clinical Social Worker," "or "Pastoral Counselor" unless licensed to do so.

5. Avoid strictly psychiatric diagnosis and interventions.

Counseling Session Policies and Procedures

1. Begin every session by explaining that you are not a professional counselor, but are offering spiritual advice, which is biblically based.

2. Always have a Bible present and prominently displayed during every counseling session.

3. Always include biblical principles, scriptures, and spiritual considerations in every counseling situation.

4. Begin and/or end every session with prayer, asking God to meet their needs, and to direct you with godly wisdom.

5. Never give any advice that is contrary to the Bible, regardless of the circumstances involved.

6. Keep records and general notes of each counseling session. For purposes of confidentiality, these records should be kept separate and secure.

7. All counseling discussions are to remain confidential. Any discussion about the counselee's situation must first have the counselee's approval before sharing their situation with any other leader. In some cases, mandatory reporting of a severe situation may apply.

8. Counseling should never be done with members of the opposite sex unless there is a third party present in the session.

9. Two adults must be present when counseling anyone under the age of 18.

10. Never enter a room, private place, or home with a child when the parents are absent.

11. Do not counsel a person for longer than six consecutive months.

Guidance for the Small Group Leader in Counseling

1. Be sure that your personal walk with the Lord is consistent and that you are blameless in the area you are counseling.

2. Be personally submitted to other pastoral leadership.

3. Be personally accountable, having a "transparent" relationship with another person.

4. Be a person of prayer and faith. Pray before, during, and after the session.

5. Always counsel from a base of inner peace. Don't counsel when you are physically or emotionally exhausted.

Practical Guidelines for the Counseling Session

1. Pray for wisdom and discernment (see Proverbs 8:11-12).

2. Always use the Bible as your source for counseling.

3. Counsel with a third person present or within view.

4. Never counsel alone with someone of the opposite sex.

5. Let your counselee know you are not a licensed professional counselor.

6. Ask questions and attentively listen to what is shared (See James 1:18-19; Proverbs 13:14).

7. Don't judge or evaluate too quickly (see Isaiah 11:2-4). The Lord is the counselor's pattern.

8. Be aware of your body language and demonstrate love (see 2 Peter 1:5-8).

9. Speak the truth in love (see Ephesians 4:14,15).

10. Guard what the counselee says confidentially, but do not commit yourself unwisely to a secretive-type confidence (see Proverbs 11:13).

11. Never act shocked at what the counselee shares with you (see Ecclesiastes 1:8-9).

12. Pray! (see 1 Thessalonians 5:17).

13. Give room for the Holy Spirit to assist you in the session.

14. Keep good records on every counseling session describing what was communicated. Include place, date and time.

The Do's and Don'ts of Good Listening

1. First and foremost, don't interrupt.

2. Be empathetic; don't condemn, argue, or patronize.

3. Stay close and involved, but don't be a space invader.

4. Talk about yourself, but don't get too familiar too fast.

5. Consider the context of the statement being made.

6. Listen with all your senses.

7. Avoid an audience or distractions of any kind.

8. Remove physical obstacles between you and a good conversation.

9. Ask open-ended questions that require more than a "yes" or "no" response.

[1] This is the City Bible Church Counseling Mission Statement developed by the All Church Leadership Team in 2001.

EVANGELISM AND THE SMALL GROUP

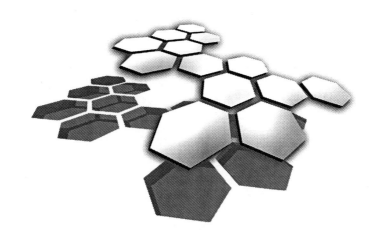

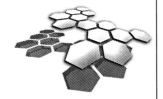

Evangelism and the Small Group
Chapter Ten

It has been said that the last words spoken by someone before they leave this earth are the most important. Jesus, in His final address to His disciples before His ascension, declared to all those who would follow Him the necessity of taking the Good News to every creature.

> *And He said to them, "Go into all the world and preach the gospel to every creature. He who believes and is baptized will be saved; but he who does not believe will be condemned. And these signs will follow those who believe: In My name they will cast out demons; they will speak with new tongues; they will take up serpents; and if they drink anything deadly, it will by no means hurt them; they will lay hands on the sick, and they will recover." So then, after the Lord had spoken to them, He was received up into heaven, and sat down at the right hand of God. And they went out and preached everywhere, the Lord working with them and confirming the word through the accompanying signs. Amen (Mark 16:15-20).*

The disciples received their marching orders from their Master. Once the instruction was communicated and understood, Christ ascended, leaving them everything they needed to accomplish His purposes. The disciples then left to accomplish the goal—reaching the world for Christ.

Jesus Came To Seek and Save the Lost

Jesus did not come just to make those in the church have a comfortable existence on planet earth. His intention was not to create a freezer to "flash freeze" His church and protect her from the world until His return, but to create an incubator that rapidly hatched out new converts.

The world is in desperate need of a Savior. Without the specific intervention of the Spirit of God into the lives of the lost, their future and destiny are hopeless! Jesus came to die for the sins of mankind, so that all who believe and follow Him might have a personal relationship with God.

> *"For the Son of Man has come to seek and to save that which was lost (Luke 19:10)."*

> *"Even so it is not the will of your Father who is in heaven that one of these little ones should perish (Matthew 18:14)."*

> *"For God so loved the world that He gave His only begotten Son, that whoever believes in Him should not perish but have everlasting life. For God did not send His Son into the world to condemn the world, but that the world through Him might be saved (John 3:16-17)."*

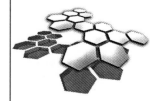

Followers of Christ are to Seek and Save the Lost

There are still more than three billion people who have not heard the gospel of Jesus Christ. In fact, every time your heart beats, someone dies. Most of them are unsaved! Every day, over 144,000 people will die, most unsaved. Every year, over 52 million people die, most unsaved.

There is an urgency to spread the gospel to a dying world. The spreading must begin with you. Revival in the nations begins with revival in you! It begins in your home, spreads to your neighborhood, and then saturates the city.

The Word of God is very clear about God's stated purposes regarding evangelism. This mission will only be accomplished through His people, the church. We must take the message of the cross to every person, in every neighborhood, in every city and nation!

> *"Indeed He says, 'It is too small a thing that You should be My Servant to raise up the tribes of Jacob, and to restore the preserved ones of Israel; I will also give You as a light to the Gentiles, **that You should be My salvation to the ends of the earth** (Isaiah 49:6)."*

> *"The LORD has made bare His holy arm in the eyes of **all the nations; and all the ends of the earth shall see the salvation of our God** (Isaiah 52:10)."*

> *"For I know their works and their thoughts. It shall be **that I will gather all nations and tongues;** and they shall come and see My glory (Isaiah 66:18)."*

> *"And He said to them, 'Go into all the world **and preach the gospel to every creature'** (Mark 16:15)."*

> *"But you shall receive power when the Holy Spirit has come upon you; and **you shall be witnesses to Me in Jerusalem, and in all Judea and Samaria, and to the end of the earth** (Acts 1:8)."*

> *"But I say, have they not heard? Yes indeed: 'Their sound has gone out **to all the earth, and their words to the ends of the world'** (Romans 10:18)."*

> *"If indeed you continue in the faith, grounded and steadfast, and are not moved away from the hope of the gospel which you heard, which was preached **to every creature under heaven,** of which I, Paul, became a minister (Colossians 1:23)"*

Evangelism in Small Groups

As we enter the new millennium, it is evident that a global awakening is taking place regarding small groups and evangelism. The church is being mobilized into small ministry centers throughout all cities, reaching into the lives of those that would never consider visiting a church building. This principle is bringing back the emphasis and growth tool used by the first century church (see Acts 16:15,32-24, 40; 18:7-8; 21:8).

A Balanced Perspective: Quality and Quantity

God desires that His Church grow both in quality and quantity. He never intended the Church to focus primarily on pastoral care, relationships, teaching, and counseling. On the flip side, He also never intended the church to abandon the sheep and their needs, and spend all of the resources and energies on reaching lost people. The fact of the matter is that He wants both! God's desire is to have a "quantity of quality."

The book of Acts models the pattern of the New Testament church and leaves a clear blueprint as to the balance between numerical growth and spiritual growth. The following diagram will help in portraying this God-given plan:

Numerical Growth in the Book of Acts		Spiritual Growth in the Book of Acts	
1:15	120 were meeting	1:14	They all joined together
2:41	3,000 were added	2:1-4	They were filled with the Holy Spirit
4:4	5,000 men were aded	2:42	Continued in Apostle's doctrine
5:14	A great number added	2:46	Continued to meet together
6:1	Number of disciples increasing	4:24	Lifted up voices in one accord
6:7	Disciples increased rapidly	4:32	All believers were of one heart and mind
8:5-24	Revival in Samaria	12:34	Word spread through the entire region
9:32-42	Conversions in Lydda and Sharon	13:49	Word continued to increase and spread
11:21-26	Many conversions in Antioch	13:52	Disciples filled with joy and Holy Spirit
13:43,44	Many followed Paul	16:5	Churches strengthened in the faith
14:20,21	Large number of disciples	17:11	Examined Scriptures every day
16:5	Galatian churches grew daily	19:20	Word of the Lord spread widely and grew in power
17:4	Large number		
17:12	Many believed		

As leaders, we need to be increasingly cognizant that we don't have to sacrifice quality for quantity. Healthy small group churches are growing churches. It is a part of our genetic make-up. It is in this cyclical process that we fulfill the vision of this house and the plan of God to "Go into all the world, **preach the gospel, and make disciples** of all nations" (see Matthew 28:20).

Imparting and Sustaining a "Harvesting Gene"

Each leader plays a key role in motivating those in the small group in evangelism. However, for us to be able to impart a heart for the lost into our leaders, we must have this as an everyday part of our own lives. It is through your living example that you will be able to impart and sustain a harvesting gene into your leaders.

Here are six practical steps to consider in maintaining a harvest mindset as a small group leader:

1. **Possess It:** You must contend for it, as it is not what you confess, but what you possess that counts.

2. **Pray It:** Make it a daily part of your prayer life, and ask the Lord to stir you in evangelism. Take that opportunity whenever it presents itself to pray this over those in your small group as well.

3. **Discuss It:** It has been said, "you get what you preach." Take the time to discuss evangelism ideas in every meeting.

4. **Encourage It:** People need constant encouragement, especially when it comes to evangelism. Encourage those in your group toward every evan-

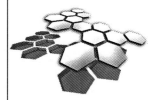

gelistic effort that is put forth.

5. **Assist It:** Get involved whenever your church is hosting some form of outreach.

6. **Model It:** Jesus led by example, we should do likewise. Look for opportunities to bring your friends and neighbors to your small group meeting as well.

Three Ways to Conduct Outreaches with the Small Group

As you move forward in fulfilling the vision of reaching your region for Christ, outreaches are a key ingredient to the success and future of the small group ministry. Here are some ways in which your small group may be involved in evangelism.

1. **Church-Initiated Outreaches:** Your church may be involved in ongoing outreaches that are planned for the entire church, as well as specific outreaches for the small groups.

2. **Small Group-Initiated Outreaches:** At times, the small group will initiate its own outreach event. The goal is to give each leader and small group the freedom to pursue their own burdens and ideas in reaching the lost. Although this is not an exhaustive list, it may give you some ideas:

- Barbecues or Potlucks
- Neighborhood Block Party
- Special Holiday Gatherings
- Gospel Video
- Serving Neighbors
- Free Car Wash for Neighborhood
- Change Batteries in Smoke Alarms
- Potted Plant Giveaways
- Sweeping Sidewalks
- Sunday Morning Paper and Coffee
- Ice Cream Socials
- SuperBowl Chili Outreach
- Picnics, Hikes, Outings
- *Ultimate Journey* Course
- Leaf-raking Parties
- Lawn Care Outreach
- Prayer Evangelism Door to Door
- Gutter Cleaning
- Graffiti Cleaning Party
- Collecting Christmas Trees

3. **Individual-Initiated Outreach:** This is by far the most effective means of evangelism. Eighty-six percent of all people that ever come to Christ and stay in the local church come through a relational contact with a neighbor, friend, relative or co-worker. This type of evangelism is also not restricted to other "event-oriented" outreaches but can take place seven days a week. As a small group leader, you should be continually encouraging your group members to motivate each person to be a daily witness.

Inviting New People to the Small Group

The small group is one of the primary means by which to bring new people into relationship with Christ, His church, and His cause. Each meeting, believers should be encouraged to invite friends and neighbors to the small group meeting.

One principle used by many leaders who teach on small groups is the "open chair" principle. Here are some ideas taken from Bill Donahue's book, *Leading Life-Changing Small Groups*.[1] Take the time to train your small group leaders to follow these concepts regularly.

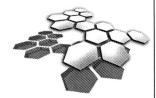

Step One: Before You Begin Inviting New Members

1. Involve everyone in the process. Each person in a small group should invite people to the group.

2. Teach your group each week about the "open chair" and its importance.

3. Regularly pray for God to fill the "open chair."

4. Develop a list of potential members to fill the chair.

5. Provide ongoing outreaches that will attract new people.

Step Two: How to Invite New Members

1. Develop relationships prior to the group meeting.

2. Explain the vision of the small group to the potential member.

3. Try to bridge relationships with others in the group before bringing them to the group.

4. Explain the format of the group, so there are no surprises.

5. Offer to give the person a ride, or even go out to eat before or after the meeting.

6. Encourage them to bring another family member or friend.

Creating a Visitor-Friendly Atmosphere in the Small Group

The experience of visiting a small group can be awkward for a new person. It can be compared to jumping off an overpass into the fast lane of a freeway, hoping not to be run over by oncoming traffic. Since the small group is a place where seekers will visit, it is important to discuss with the group, on an on-going basis, the need to maintain a friendly atmosphere. Here are some recommendations.

1. Make sure the visitor is getting attention at all times before and after the official meeting. Don't let group members form cliques and alienate the new person.

2. Introduce the new person to the rest of the group and let them know how excited the group is to have them present.

3. Be aware of any needs that the visitor may have and attempt to meet those needs.

4. Explain each part of the meeting and reasons why the group is doing certain things (worship, offering, message, etc.).

5. Use Bible translations that are relevant to the visitor (New Living Translation, New King James, New International Version, etc.).

6. Don't force the visitor to speak or share their opinion if they want to just observe.

7. Avoid using "Christianese." Phrases like "our church is on fire" or, "I'm standing on the Word" or "gotta' get plugged in" are confusing to the visitor.

8. Be transparent and honest. Let them see that Christians are real people with similar trials and struggles.

9. Ask them if there are any needs that the group can pray for, believing God for a miracle on their behalf.

Welcoming New People to the Small Group

There are many ways to make a person feel welcome and special. An established plan for welcoming visitors to a group will bring many back for the second and third visit. Here are some suggestions for making your small group a desired destination for visitors.

1. Have group members notify the leader or assistant that they are bringing a visitor to the group.

2. Put together an informal gift to give to every visitor who attends (cookies, booklet, a worship tape, etc). Have a few backup gifts for unexpected visitors.

3. Always greet your new guests at the door. If you know the name of the visitor, use their name to greet them.

4. Introduce your visitor to others in the group. Encourage them to get to know each other.

5. Assist the visitor in finding a seat. They may feel awkward, not knowing where to sit.

6. At the beginning of the meeting, introduce them to the entire group. Share a few comments about the person, and mention whose guest they are.

7. Give the visitor the gift and have each person welcome them.

8. At the conclusion of the meeting, thank them for coming and encourage them to return again. Give them the time and date for the next meeting. Ask if they would allow you to call them sometime in the near future to remind them about the next meeting.

Small Group Prayer Walking

Our future is in the hands of God and influenced by prayer-intercession. One of the small group functions is to pray for the lost people around us. One option could be that small groups learn to pray for their neighborhood street by street, and home by home. This same principle can be applied to the workplace or the school campus as well. We call this activity prayer walking with divine purpose, to bless places and people through prayer. If your group chooses to prayer-walk, the following section will assist you in planning a successful prayer-walk.

Prayer Walking Defined

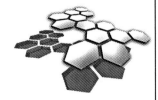

1. Prayer walking is simply what it sounds like—walking while praying with specific, directed, intentional prayer in a very non-religious and non-traditional manner.

2. Prayer-walking is on-site praying, allowing God to work with us and through us as His touch point to release His power and compassion.

3. Prayer-walking is focused praying—prayer for others on location, focusing our intercessory prayer on neighborhoods, homes, and people.

4. Prayer-walking is praying in the very places where you expect your prayer to be heard and answered, and for God to be glorified.

5. Prayer-walking is focused on releasing God's blessing over the area, praying for His grace, mercy, and redeeming love to be released over every person and every place.

6. Prayer-walking is part of the believer's responsibility in discovering the fruit of the future, seeing our region filled with God's future blessings.

Prayer-Walking Scriptures

*Genesis 13:17 "Arise, **walk** in the land through its length and its width, for I give it to you."*

*Joshua 1:3 "Every place that the sole of your foot will **tread** upon I have given you, as I said to Moses."*

*Deuteronomy 11:24 "Every place on which the sole of your foot **treads** shall be yours."*

*Deuteronomy 1:36 "… Except Caleb the son of Jephunneh; he shall see it, and to him and his children I am giving the land on which he **walked**, because he wholly followed the LORD."*

*Joshua 18:8 "Then the men arose to go away; and Joshua charged those who went to survey the land, saying, 'Go, **walk** through the land, survey it, and come back to me, that I may cast lots for you here before the LORD in Shiloh.'"*

*1 Chronicles 17:8 "And I have been with you **wherever you have gone,** and have cut off all your enemies from before you, and have made you a name like the name of the great men who are on the earth."*

*Matthew 9:35 "Then Jesus **went about** all the cities and villages, teaching in their synagogues, preaching the gospel of the kingdom, and healing every sickness and every disease among the people."*

*Luke 10:1-3 "After these things the Lord appointed seventy others also, and sent them two by two before His face into **every city and place** where He Himself **was about to go.** Then He said to them, 'The harvest truly is great, but the laborers are few; therefore pray the Lord of the harvest to send out laborers into His harvest. Go your way; behold, I send you out as lambs among wolves.'"*

The Purpose of Prayer-Walking

1. **To Move the Church into the Community** (see Acts 2:46-47).
    Prayer-walking helps to get the church outside its buildings and into the community in spiritual and numerical strength. Although the primary aim is not evangelism, it gets people asking what you are doing. Sometimes a passerby may ask you to pray for them. God will guide you even as He guided Philip in Acts 8:26-38.

2. **To Increase Our Awareness of the Needs Around Us** (see Matthew 9: 20-22). Prayer-walking "earths" our heavenly intercessions. Many Christians pray for their neighborhood without actually encountering it. We do not know what is there because we do not do the legwork to find out. Through prayer walking, Christians can discover streets and places they never knew existed, including local clubs and institutions they had previously ignored.

3. **To Make Divinely Appointed Contact with the Lost** (see Psalm 2:8).
    In prayer walking you have the opportunity to meet new people. Occasionally these contacts can lead to conversions. Sometimes you may feel led to witness to a passerby the Lord has laid on your heart. They may be saved or healed or both! Prayer walking provides that crucial ingredient—being there!

4. **To Invade Satan's Territory Humbly by God's Grace** (see Acts 17:15-34). Discern evil carefully with a heightened sensitivity to spiritual battle as you intercede on the streets. Prayer walking takes us bodily and spiritually into territories where Satan has vested interests. We become aware of the numerous altars in the neighborhood. We also notice the different religious places of worship that are otherwise ignored.

5. **To Redeem the Time** (see Ephesians 5:16).
    Prayer-walking releases us from the activities that rob us of our prayer time. In spite of the benefits of cars and modern appliances, we still complain of having no time to pray. The reason is simply that we are surrounded by "time robbers." The television, the telephone, the newspapers and magazines are examples of "time robbers" which steal frightening amounts of our time with all the subtlety of a pickpocket. You do not realize the time is gone until you need it for something important like prayer.

6. **To Penetrate Our Streets with Righteousness** (see Acts 19:17-20).
    Getting righteous people out praying on the streets as a regular part of life is one of the most effective ways of freeing our towns from the scourge of robbery, rape, and violence. Through such prayers, the church can change the balance of spiritual power and make our streets safer places for people in the neighborhood.

7. **To Bless Every Place Systematically** (see Proverbs 11:11).
    Where the blessing of God is, there can be no darkness. One principle given to the disciples by Jesus in Luke 10 was to bless anyone they came into contact with as they entered the city. We can also pray for God's blessing to come to our neighbor's life, which in turn works to remove evil.

8. **To Tear Down Spiritual Strongholds with Wisdom** (see 2 Corinthians 10:4). As you continue prayer-walking on a regular basis, you will find the

Lord imparting to you specifics regarding your prayer targets. This allows you to be able to pray more specifically against the stronghold in the area with greater wisdom and effectiveness.

9. **To Pray Patiently and Consistently for Spiritual Awakening** (see Exodus 22:30). The enemy has blinded the eyes of unbelievers so that they can't see the light. Our city is filled with blinded people. We have learned from previous revivals that praying specifically for spiritual awakening has been a key ingredient in bringing forth the harvest.

10. **To Pray for the Needs of Others with Compassion and Faith** (see Luke 10:30-35). Jesus spent most of His public ministry reaching out to the poor, sick, lost, abused, accused, and accursed. Over forty times in the Gospels, He ministered to the physical and emotional needs before the spiritual. One of the most effective ways to reach people is through their felt need. Prayer will help to open the door so that you can minister to other needs later on.

Planning a Prayer-Walk with a Small Group

Here are few suggestions to assist you in making your prayer-walking efforts a success.

1. Determine the area that you will pray for. Choose an area that is convenient for your group and an area that you can walk through repeatedly.

2. Assign a member of the group to research names of home and business owners in the designated area.

3. Have a plan. Inform each person of the strategy and give a short briefing before heading out.

4. Set an allotted time. Teams will head out and meet back for a reporting session.

5. Plan ongoing prayer walks. The area you choose needs constant prayer saturation in order to see a breakthrough.

6. Give each team a specific set of directions and boundaries for their walk. This may be done by giving a specific street or block to each team.

7. If possible, identify Christians or churches in the area and pray for God's special blessing on them as you walk.

8. Don't prayer-walk in large groups. A maximum of three people per team is ideal.

Personal Preparation for Prayer-Walking

A few principles should be communicated and activated before your prayer-walk.

1. Spend time in prayer and worship before prayer-walking.

2. Pray specifically against a spirit of fear, doubt and disbelief.

3. Encourage and speak faith into the group. Let them know their prayers will make a difference.

Positive Suggestions for Prayer-Walking

1. Pray for a release of God's presence over the each household.

2. Pray for individuals by name whenever possible.

3. Pray with a spirit of faith and expectancy.

4. Pray for discernment.

5. Exercise wisdom and self-control.

6. Pray quietly and don't draw attention to yourselves.

7. Keep walking; don't stop in front of a house to pray.

8. Be friendly and cordial with anyone you meet.

9. Stop and talk with someone if they want to converse.

10. Be respectful of other's private property.

11. Stay on the sidewalks and streets; don't cut across anyone's yard.

[1] Bill Donahue, *Leading Life-Changing Small Groups*, Zondervan Publishing House, 1996, p.158.

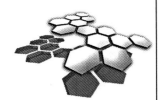

ASSIMILATION
IN THE
SMALL GROUP

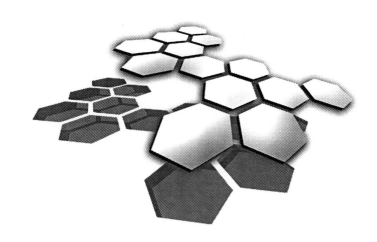

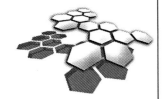

Assimilation in the Small Group
Chapter Eleven

As we push forward into the 21st Century, there is high expectation in churches all over the world for global harvest. Currently there are over 178,000 people giving their lives to Christ daily. This is truly a great day to be alive. Although these are great numbers to get excited about, the real measuring rod should be the number that are being assimilated into the life of local churches, not just those praying a salvation prayer at an altar. Jesus said, "Go and make disciples," not "go and make decisions." As a 21st century, New Testament church, our focus must be to make healthy, active, reproducing disciples, not weekend warriors.

As we anticipate multitudes being saved in our church and in the churches regionally, we must do our part in building strong "nets" in which to contain and bring in the "catch." In the Gospels there are two accounts in which Jesus went fishing with the disciples. In both cases many fish were caught. However, there is a noticeable difference in the number of fish that were contained. In one case, nets were breaking, in the other the nets stayed intact.

> *Luke 5:6 "And this time their nets were so full that **they began to tear**."*

> *John 21:11 "So Simon Peter went out and dragged the net ashore. By his count there were one hundred fifty-three large fish; and yet **the net hadn't torn**."*

It is the Lord's will that we build a church assimilation structure that can contain the "catch" God brings our way. One of the primary nets are small groups. As the harvest continues to increase, the small groups will play a critical role in sharing the load of assimilation and discipleship. In order for this to happen, each leader must make sure that they understand the principles and goals of assimilation.

Assimilation is _____.
The Bible compares evangelism to fishing. Jesus said in Luke 5:10, *"Do not be afraid. From now on you will catch men."* We are all called to be fishers of men. However, fishing in biblical times is much different than our western perception of fishing. Fishing was often done in the cold raging seas, working all hours of the night, fighting currents and high tides, trying to grab nets filled with smelly fish.

This is an appropriate analogy of what it is like to work with new converts. We can never expect to get a thousand dollars of results with a dime's worth of effort. We will get out of the harvesting process what we put into it. As a small group leader, count on working hard in the harvest. The challenge may be tough, but the benefits are out of this world!

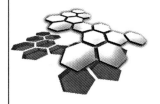

Evangelism is a _____.

Evangelism is a process, which includes pre-conversion, conversion, and post-conversion effort. It is the process from sinner to saint! Many have been deceived into believing that evangelism takes place at some church service or outreach event. They think that once someone prays the prayer, evangelism was successful. However, there are three main ingredients in the complete process, as illustrated by the iceberg diagram below. All three components are critical to the success of evangelism.

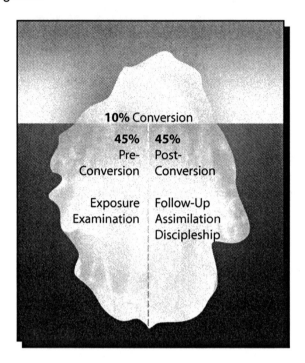

1. **Pre-Conversion:** The average person comes into contact with the gospel approximately seven to ten times before making a commitment to follow Christ. This process can take years. Therefore, group members should work on building long-term relationships with pre-believers and attempt to expose them to the gospel message over a period of time.

2. **Conversion:** The conversion experience is the most crucial part of the process. All of the angels in heaven rejoice when one soul is saved. We should be excited and thankful that the Lord has used us to usher someone into the Kingdom of God, but should never stop working with the person to see them discipled. Conversion is not the end of the process, but the turning point.

3. **Post-Conversion:** The discipleship process will vary depending on a variety of circumstances. Some new converts will be ready to lead a small group after only a year, while others may take ten to fifteen years! Their desire to move forward, their attitude, and the excess baggage they have brought into the Kingdom all have a bearing on the outcome of the post-conversion process.

Assimilation is the _____.

The post-conversion process typically provides the greatest challenge to new converts. Many have major adjustments and changes that need to take place in their lives, and few Christians are willing to pay the price of sacrifice to walk the new convert through the many months of the discipleship process.

Assimilating a new believer requires much more than seeing the individual attend a New Life Class. This process requires getting intimately involved in their lives and standing by their side through every challenge they face. Often this requires working with someone three or four times a week! Because the process requires such an effort, some are unwilling to pay the price of truly discipling new believers.

As church leaders, we are committed to working with people to assist them in becoming all they are meant to be in the Kingdom of God. We are willing and able to pay the price of bringing people from the "gutter-most to the uttermost." We trust that as a small group leader, you will also labor with us and join in this worthy cause of making saints out of sinners!

Our Church Assimilation Structure

The process by which we move people from visiting to belonging is defined as "assimilation." With that definition being our goal, our job is not complete until we see each individual reach their full potential and final destination as an active, reproducing member of our local church. This process requires the support of every department working closely together to make sure the assimilation process of every person God brings our way is successful.

The involvement of the small group leader is critical in this process. As you care for your group, one priority is to assist each person in moving forward in the maturing process. Therefore, it is important that each leader understand the assimilation process of the church and use it as a tool to develop healthy, active, reproducing members in their group.

Below is our church's assimilation structure:*

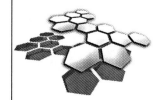

*See Appendix page 170 for City Bible Church's example.

Four Assimilation Duties of a Small Group Leader

The assimilation structure has been designed to contain the "catch" God brings our way. Small groups are a primary component of that structure. As the harvest continues to increase, the small groups play a critical role in sharing the load of assimilation and discipleship. In order for this to happen, each leader must make sure that they understand and apply the principles and goals of assimilation.

_____ *into the Small Group*

The small group becomes a major hub of all assimilation activity. It is in this group that each person will find the relationships necessary for long-term support, and a place to serve using their God-given gifts. Work to build the group by reaching people in the following ways:

1. Invite a friend.

2. Attend a small group-sponsored outreach.

3. Meeting visitors to your church.

4. Meet people at the altar during a weekend service.

5. Meet people before or after a weekend service in the lobby or sanctuary.

6. Call all those within your area who do not attend a small group.

7. Work with other outreach ministries in the church.

8. Get involved in the "adopt-a-family" concept (targeting one particular person or family and befriending them by calling them, praying for them, inviting them to a meal, on a regular basis, etc.).

_____ *in the Small Group*

Another way people are added to the small group is through salvation. With each small group focusing on reaching neighbors and friends, there will be those who give their life to Christ as a direct result of the small group and not a church event or service. We hope this type of evangelism will become the predominant way that people are added to the church, not the exception.

Throughout this chapter, there has been great emphasis on making disciples, not just decisions. Your leadership is crucial in guiding the people within your small group to assist in discipling new converts or rededications. There are three ways in which you can disciple someone within your small group:

A. **The Small Group Leader:** If your group is small, or just getting started, you may have the desire and time to work with the new convert yourself to ensure they are receiving proper care and attention.

B. **An Assigned Discipler:** There may be an individual in a small group that has a passion to work with new converts. You may want to have your own evangelist/assimilation person in your group to help with the evangelism, discipleship and assimilation of all new people in your group.

C. **The Person Who Brought the New Convert:** One of the most effective ways to follow up a new convert is through an existing relationship. Although this means of discipleship can be fruitful, it can also be disastrous

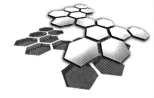

if the existing acquaintance does not have the desire or training to work with the new convert. You, as their leader, may need to make a judgment call.

Using _____ in the Small Group

Each small group leader should have church approved follow-up materials available at every meeting.[1] These materials are designed to assist a discipler in the follow-up process.

Once someone has prayed to receive Christ in the small group, have the person responsible for discipling the individual do the following:

1. Find a quiet place where there will be minimal distractions.

2. Pray with the person for any specific needs they may have.

3. Discuss the importance of the decision that they have just made.

4. Answer any questions or explain any unclear thoughts.

5. Open up the follow-up materials approved by the church and discuss with new convert.

6. Encourage them to begin reading a minimum of two chapters in the Bible a day. You may ask if they have a Bible. If not, you may obtain a Bible from a local bookstore, or your church office, if available.

7. Set up a follow-up appointment to get together as soon as possible. The ideal is within twenty-four hours. Let them know that you want to spend more time with them to pray, discuss their decision to follow Christ, next steps that will be helpful in their new relationship with Christ, as well as to get to know them a little better.

Closing _____ in Small Groups: Small Group Care

Part of the assimilation process is to make sure those who are in a small group do not fall through cracks of the church and disappear. This part of caring for your small group is just as important as dealing with new converts. We do not want to bring the masses in through the front door only to find out that our back door is wide open as well. Because every person matters to God, they must also matter to us.

The primary means for keeping people in your small group is *care*. If each person knows you care for them, they will remain faithful to you and the group. The best way to show that you care is through frequent contact with each person in your small group. Here are some general guidelines to help you implement "small group care" into your group:

1. Use a small group attendance list as a calling and reference sheet.

2. Set aside some time at least once a month, when you can make calls and not be interrupted.

3. Call each person in the group and spend a few minutes talking with them. Make the conversation very relational. Do not to use the call to remind them about the next meeting or to ask them to do something for the small

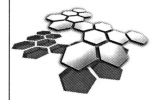

group. This call is designed to build relationships and to care for their needs.

4. Pray for every person and ask if they have any needs or concerns. Spend a few minutes agreeing in prayer with them for their need.

5. If it is at all possible, meet any need you can by using the resources provided to you as a small group leader. You may also contact your leaders to assist you with the needs that arise.

6. If there are any serious counseling needs, crisis situations, or issues that are beyond your ability, contact your pastoral leadership immediately for additional assistance.

[1] City Bible Church uses the "Commitment Packet" available through City Christian Publishing. It contains the Book of John, three *Eternity* booklets used for presenting the Gospel, follow-up, and water baptism.

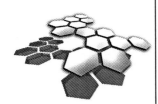

THE INGREDIENTS OF A SMALL GROUP MEETING

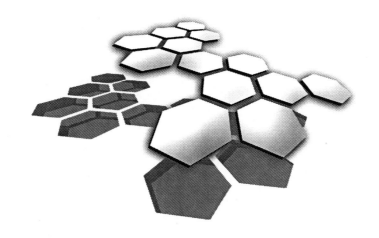

The Ingredients of a Small Group Meeting
Chapter Twelve

The key to a great award-winning recipe is making sure to have all the proper ingredients. Without the right type and proportion of each ingredient, any recipe can turn into a disaster. When it comes to small groups, there are also ingredients necessary for its success.

Preparation for the Small Group Meeting

As you look toward your meetings, you should take steps to make each meeting as successful as possible. One of the most important ingredients to success is preparation. Your people will only get something out of your meeting if you put something into your meeting.

Each meeting may have a different emphasis which will dictate the content of the meeting. Some groups may focus on a Bible study, whereas other groups may have pre-designated materials, or a special focus. Listed below are some general ideas to assist in planning a typical small group meeting. Please review and use as it applies to your group setting.

1. Look up relevant Scriptures and meditate on them.

2. Think through each discussion question and write down any thoughts that come to your mind.

3. Gather any special items that are needed for the meeting.

4. Call the person in charge of worship (if worship is a part of your group) and let them know the theme of the meeting. Ask them to gather songs that enhance the meeting's topic.

5. Look for opportunities to assign portions of the meeting to other individuals in the group. These can be discussed at your planning meeting with your leaders.

6. If you will be out of town, call your assistant and make sure they have all the notes and any instructions necessary to have a great meeting.

7. Call your host and see if they have any requests or needs.

8. If one person is in charge of refreshments, make sure they contact others to bring refreshments.

9. If one person is in charge of the children, call and make sure they have a plan for the meeting.

10. Call everyone in your group the week of the meeting and make sure they know the time and the location of the meeting.

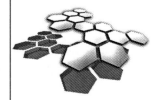

11. Call any new people recently given to you by your leaders. Encourage them to come with their family or any friends.

General Guidelines for the Small Group

These guidelines may be affected by the different needs present in each group, the various personalities and chemistry within the group, and times when the Holy Spirit may change the direction of the meeting. The small group meeting should have a basic structure, with room to move, grow and be creative. Here are some general guidelines you may follow:

1. We want to encourage every small group leader to clearly communicate the behavior guidelines toward the host and their home at the first meeting. This does not apply to groups that may meet in a public place, or another setting.

2. Each member of the group will be responsible for helping to create a Christ-like atmosphere of love and acceptance.

3. Every person will be asked to honor and respect the hosts and their home.

4. The group leader will have the spiritual authority for the entire group .

5. For those groups that have children, the parent has the authority for the behavior of their own children. Everyone will be asked to provide support to other parents and children.

6. Any conflicts with the children will be discussed with parents and the group leader.

7. The hosts have the right to set "House Rules" for behavior in their home. The leader and hosts should discuss this before the first meeting so that the rules can be announced.

8. The entire group, including any children, should have an agreement about the rules of the group.

Suggested House Rule Guidelines

1. Do not run inside the house.

2. Do not jump on or put your feet on the furniture.

3. Do not use household equipment or toys without permission.

4. Do not go into the bedrooms or other rooms of the house without permission.

5. Help clean up messes before leaving.

6. Ask permission to use the bathroom.

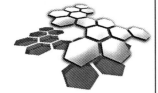

7. Do not eat any refreshments before the set time.

8. Children are to stay with parents during refreshment time, unless the host says otherwise.

Components of an Effective Small Group Meeting

As you begin to develop your small group team and strategy, there are some components that you should study before making any final decisions.

Choosing the Right Host Home

The environment of a group meeting is crucial to its success. There should be a friendly, warm, relaxed atmosphere in every meeting. There are many places to meet, but if you choose to meet in a home, you may want to consider having more than one home as an option. Consider the following suggestions in choosing a host home(s).

Size: The host home should be large enough to accommodate a good-sized group (12 to 20 people). Make sure there is a large room in the home where the entire group can meet at one time. Some small groups may decide to rotate locations between the different members. Make sure that the homes where your group meets have adequate room.

Accessibility: The host home should be easy to find, so people will not get lost (this would apply especially for first time visitors). Not only is the location important, but also the accessibility to the home itself is important. Homes with steep drives, muddy areas, lack of outside lighting, for example, may hinder people's desire to attend the small group.

Appearance: The host home should be appealing and comfortable. The home should not be messy, dirty, or in disrepair. Make sure it is orderly and clean.

Atmosphere: The hosts should create an atmosphere of safety and friendliness.

Choosing the Right Hosts

Many small group leaders or assistants choose to be the hosts as well. However, it is ideal to have a separate host home. Sometimes people are willing to lead, but their home does not have adequate room to host a small group. If you choose to use a host and their home, here are some tips to assist in the selection process.

1. Hosts should be friendly and hospitable.

2. Hosts should enjoy being a part of a small group.

3. Hosts should be people who manage their children well (if any).

4. Hosts should believe that every person matters to God.

5. Hosts should desire to see God's presence dwell in their home.

6. Hosts should not be overly concerned about unknown visitors coming to their home.

7. Hosts should be gracious about having many people in their home at one time.

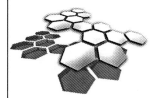

Choosing the Right Worship Leader

Many groups make worship a regular part of the group gathering. On some occasions there may not be anyone in the group that is gifted on an instrument. In such cases, worship without instruments or using a CD player will suffice. It is better to sing without instruments or use a CD than to have someone who plays poorly, or whose life is out of order.

1. A worship leader should be living a godly life.

2. A worship leader should have a passion for the presence of God.

3. A worship leader should be submitted to the small group leader and leadership of the church.

4. A worship leader should be disciplined to learn current songs.

5. A worship leader should have an instrument that is mobile to bring to the meeting, unless one exists at the host home.

Crossing Culture Barriers in the Small Group

There is an increase in ethnic visitors to local churches and small groups. Most cities today are made up of many people-groups from other nations. As the harvest continues to increase, the number of ethnic people attending our church will also increase. The church must continue to reach across all culture barriers.

Reaching out to ethnic people can be very rewarding for the entire group. This reward comes when we are sensitive to the ways in which we can make each person belong. We have some specific ideas to help, but they are useless without building on a foundation of love and unconditional acceptance. Here are guidelines that will help you in making those from different ethnic backgrounds feel loved and welcome.

Tips That Can Help Them Adjust and Belong

1. Love them! Use all your abilities of hospitality. Make every effort to be their friend.

2. Learn to say their names the way they pronounce them.

3. Be willing to spend time listening. This may require some patience, but with time it becomes much easier to understand a different accent even when it is very strong.

4. Show interest in learning about them and their country. Ask questions about their culture, history, family, etc.

5. When they don't understand what you are saying, try to speak clearly and slowly, but not louder. Use alternate words that may be simpler.

6. When you don't understand what is being said:
   • Ask them to repeat or explain using an example.
   • Try to repeat what was said. "Is that right?" "Do I understand?"
   • Have them communicate by writing.
   • If there is still a communication problem, don't push the issue.

7. Encourage them to participate fully and even to lead in some activities. They may be shy at first, but really will enjoy being involved. It may take a few invitations, so don't give up.

8. If you sense a problem, ask direct questions gently. Don't be defensive. They may even need to share the negative things about western culture that bother them.

9. Invite them for a meal at a time where it is only them and you. Meals are a great way to bond.

Things That Can Cause Offenses

1. Talking "baby talk" or broken English in a desire to simplify the speech.

2. Giving a "too-busy" impression. We often do this without realizing it, due to the fast pace of our culture.

3. Not saying their name correctly, or not making an effort to learn the correct pronunciation.

4. A prideful, paternalistic, or imperialistic attitude (sometimes American patriotism can come across in this manner).

5. Asking questions about their country that can be received as a put-down.

6. A continual teasing about their accent or any of the differences in their culture or lifestyle. They want you to correct their English kindly, but teasing can be humiliating and tiresome.

7. Be careful about being critical of differences in behavior, child raising, or husband/wife roles that are more cultural preferences than biblical standards. This can be a puzzling area at times, and it would be good to check with others with cross-cultural experience before you express anything to them.

Refreshments in the Small Group

One of the best ways to develop and enhance relationships in your group is to have refreshments at every meeting. This could be a complete meal, a barbecue, finger foods or a simple dessert. Whatever you plan, keep it simple! Here are a few ideas:

1. Don't be afraid to ask people to bring food and supplies; don't supply everything yourself. Call and ask people to bring a special dish, napkins, paper cups, plastic forks, spoons, etc.

2. Consider the financial condition of each person. Some may not have the finances to bring something every time. You may ask them to assist in setting up the food so they are involved and not left out.

3. Consider requesting foods that can be served on napkins to avoid purchasing paper plates or washing dishes.

4. All desserts should be pre-cut before bringing to the meeting. Don't create work that will pull people from relating to others.

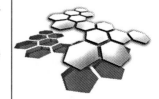

5. For those groups with children, make sure parents supervise their children during refreshment time unless the hosts allow different rules. There may also be a designated area for children.

6. The size of your group will determine the number of people bringing food.

7. If you plan a full meal (potluck) allow extra time for set up and clean up in your meeting time. Communicate this to each person when you call them before the meeting. Assign extra people to help so that the burden doesn't fall on one individual.

8. Rotate responsibilities of bringing food so that everyone is involved in serving the group.

9. Keep open communication with your hosts and make sure there are no problems during the refreshment time. Make any adjustments necessary.

10. You may want the hosts to provide hot beverages such as coffee or tea. You can reimburse them for their expenses, or they may want to donate these items as a part of their contribution to the group.

11. Follow different themes for your refreshments. Try a Mexican night, a dessert night, a pizza night, etc.

12. Be sure to give every person a minimum of three days notice to bring food so they have ample time to prepare.

13. Make it a point to thank your hosts during every meeting.

Children in the Small Group

Many small groups will have children in their meetings, although some groups may specialize in a certain age group or specific homogeneous backgrounds which may not include children.

Children are a gift from the Lord and working with children brings great rewards, and also great responsibilities—and challenges! Children are never too young to understand God's truths when presented simply, and on their level. The small group provides a unique opportunity to minister to young children in an intimate setting. This does not mean they must be in a meeting for its entire length, but as leaders, we need to show the parents and the children that each child matters to God and is important to the success of the group. Here are some options to consider as you develop your small group.

1. Children may be included in the entire group meeting. This is an age-integrated format.

2. Children participate in a portion of the meeting and then are dismissed to a separate area for special instruction.

3. Children have their own meeting in a separate room for the entire time.

Children are capable of understanding spiritual concepts and experiencing them as a reality in their own lives. Our expectations will often determine the level of their understanding. This does not mean that we are to push the child into adult responsibilities, but instruct them to be active, responsible participants in the meeting. A child can be involved in the following ways.

1. **Worship:** Children need to be trained to know what worship is and how to worship God.

2. **Prayer:** Children are very sincere about prayer. The faith of a child is exemplary. They can learn to pray for healing, for intercession, for spiritual warfare, and for forgiveness and cleansing.

3. **The Message:** Children can learn from the Word and group discussion times. If the message is clear, they will take the nuggets they receive and apply them to their daily lives.

4. **Ministry Time:** Allow children to minister to others during times of prayer. They are very capable of giving encouragement and comfort.

5. **Evangelism:** Children are often very direct and honest as they talk to others about Jesus. They can be a vital part of our effort to reach out to our community.

Tips for Teaching Children

There is a variety of great material available for you to use. You may also talk with the person who oversees children's ministry in your church. However, you may find many capable people within your group who have the desire and creativity to come up with great ideas on their own. Make sure whatever is taught to the children is first reviewed by the small group leader. Here are some tips:

1. Identify your main theme and key scripture clearly. Keep it simple.

2. Make sure everything relates to your main theme.

3. Focus on one main thought. Too many concepts will lose the attention of the children.

4. Be as animated and exciting as possible. This is necessary to retain their attention.

5. Use visual aids.

6. Involve the children as much as you can. Get them to respond to the lesson.

7. Change the pace frequently. Use discussion, a game, a song, etc.

General Guidelines for Working with Children in the Small Group

1. The leader has the oversight and responsibility for the entire group.

2. You may choose one person to oversee the children's ministry in the group. Although one may be in charge, there must always be at least two people working with the children at all times to protect against any child abuse situation.

3. The group leader must approve anyone who works with children. Those with unknown or questionable character should not work with the children.

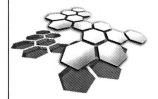

4. The parents are responsible for the behavior of their own children.

5. Parents are to change their own child's diaper. This should be done in the bathroom and not in an open room where other people are visiting.

6. In a darkened room, such as for videos, children are not allowed to sit on anyone's lap except their parent's, unless the parents give specific permission.

7. If there is a conflict, the parents and the leader should discuss it.

8. The hosts have the right to establish "House Rules" regarding children and the group.

9. The group members should understand and agree together on the rules of the group. The following section will give you some suggestions.

Children's Agreement Ideas

1. Children are to be respectful to all adults.

2. Children will participate in the group at whatever level decided by the group leader.

3. Children will not talk about sensitive family matters with others in the group.

4. Children will obey the established "House Rules."

5. Children will not fight or exclude any other children in the group.

Adult Agreement Ideas

1. Parents will look after their own children during the entire meeting unless the children are in a separate room. If there is a problem with a child, the parents will be notified to come and deal with the child.

2. Adults will be patient with all children in the group.

3. Parents will assist in supporting all "House Rules".

4. Parents will not talk about children without their permission first.

5. The leaders will not ignore children in the group.

6. Adults will be sensitive to the time of the meeting, not leaving children in their children's group too long.

7. Adults will attempt to learn each child's name and make them feel important.

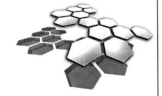

Creating and Sustaining a Holy Spirit Atmosphere in the Small Group

The entire human race is affected and impacted by "atmosphere." Wherever people are, the atmosphere that surrounds them has an astonishing effect on their lives and destiny. Unfortunately, those who are not Christians do not have the ability to create or change the atmosphere around them; they can only respond to it. As Christians, we have the ability, with the guidance and participation of the Holy Spirit, to actually change any negative atmosphere that surrounds us into "open heavens!"

Discerning different spiritual atmospheres is a part of the believer's responsibility. The spiritual atmospheres we encounter have a profound effect upon our mind, will, emotions, and spirit. The atmosphere to which a person submits has the power to change and shape them positively, or corrupt them.

As a small group leader, one of your primary goals is to create an "open heavens" atmosphere on your life, your family and your group. Without the presence of the Holy Spirit in a group, you don't have a small group meeting! The best speech to a believer or non-believer will never change their soul. That happens only through the miracle-working power of the presence of God, found in a group with the right atmosphere.

***Atmosphere* defined:** A pervading or surrounding influence or spirit (God or devil), general mood (good or bad), or environment (dirty or clean).

> *To be in the presence of the Lord is to be revived. When a community of believers is brought low before the presence of the Lord, when the very air that they breathe appears to be supercharged with the sense of His presence—this is the beginning of revival. It is revival!*
> —*J. Edwin Orr*

Working to create a positive, powerful atmosphere within your small group should be an ongoing aggressive process. In a Bible-based, Holy Spirit-led group, there are many possibilities of how the group atmosphere may feel. For example, there may be excitement, joy, victory, healing, or salvation.

A church should be committed to developing, maintaining and increasing the following twelve atmospheres within corporate gatherings, small groups, families, individual lives, and ultimately in neighborhoods, the community, and the nations!

1. **An Atmosphere of *Open Heavens***
   No spiritual hindrances allowed—breakthrough

2. **An Atmosphere of *Unified Expectancy***
   No "business as usual" meetings

3. **An Atmosphere of *Supernatural Surprises***
   It is no common, ordinary God we serve.

4. **An Atmosphere where *Everyone can Receive***
   No limitations allowed to be placed on anyone

5. **An Atmosphere where *People are Important***
   No person is undervalued here.

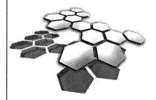

6. **An Atmosphere of *Victorious Living is Possible***
   No defeatist spirit; God is able to deliver at anytime.

7. **An Atmosphere of *Reaching Our City***
   No "hold the fort" philosophy; we attack and take no prisoners

8. **An Atmosphere of *Financial Blessing***
   No excuses or apologies; God is good and He desires to bless and provide for His work.

9. **An Atmosphere of *Communion***
   Where the voice of God is heard clearly

10. **An Atmosphere of *Faith***
    No pessimism about the future; God is in control

11. **An Atmosphere of *Vision***
    Where people see the invisible and do the impossible

12. **An Atmosphere of *Worship***
    Where the river of God is released in fullness

Worship in the Small Group

The breath of life and vitality in your small group comes from your commitment and devotion towards worshipping God. When God's people hunger for Spirit-filled, exuberant worship, it produces an atmosphere that changes hearts and lives. Consider the following quotes and Scriptures concerning worship.

"For we are the true circumcision who worship in the Sprit of God and glory in Christ Jesus (Philippians 3:3)."

"Be filled (continuously) with the Spirit, speaking to one another in psalms and hymns and spiritual songs, singing and making melody with your heart to the Lord; always giving thanks for all things (Ephesians 5:18-19)."

"Let the Word of Christ richly dwell within you, with all wisdom, teaching and admonishing one another with psalms and hymns and spiritual songs, singing with thankfulness in your hearts to God (Colossians 3:16)."

Quotes

"Worship is the metabolism of the Christian life."—Jaraslav Pelikan

"It is by its worship that the church lives."—J.J. von Allmen

"It is there that its heart beats (the church). Where there is a crisis of worship you will find a widespread crisis of faith."—Marianne H. Micks

Biblical Worship Ingredients

As a small group leader you may be very familiar with expressive, vibrant worship. However, you may have people in your group who come from a different religious background, or a visitor who does not understand the style of worship many enjoy so freely. There may be times where you will need to discuss these worship components with those who have questions. Here are some Scriptures to assist you in explaining why these components are part of our worship times.

- ❑ Singing (see Psalm 30:4, 47:6, 95:1; Ephesians 5:19).

- ❑ Lifting Hands (see Psalm 63:4, 134:2; 1 Timothy 2:8).

- ❑ Singing a New Song (see Psalm 40:3, 96:1, 98:1, 149:1).

- ❑ Clapping (see Psalm 47:1, 98:8).

- ❑ Dancing (see Psalm 149:3, 150:4).

- ❑ Shouting (see Psalm 35:27).

- ❑ Standing (see Deuteronomy 10:8; Psalm 134:1, 135:2).

- ❑ Kneeling (see Psalm 95:6; Luke 22:41; Acts 9:40, 20:36).

- ❑ Speaking in Tongues (see 1 Corinthians 14:2,5,18,27).

- ❑ Using Instruments (see 2 Samuel 6:5; Psalm, 33:2-3, 144:9, 150:3-5).

Practical Tips for Worship in the Small Group

1. Pick songs that are simple to learn and easy to sing.

2. Be sensitive to the time.

3. Be sensitive to the Holy Spirit. Allow time to meditate on God and soak in His presence.

4. Be sensitive to visitors. If they seem uncomfortable, spend a minute explaining the different components of worship found in the Bible.

5. Include children and teens in the worship team.

6. Use songs that are in the "flow" with current congregational use.

7. Use handouts with the words of the songs, if possible. Lead sheets with words and chords may be available from your music department.

8. Don't allow the instruments to be too loud or distracting.

9. Get the group involved. Talk to them. Encourage them. Get them excited!

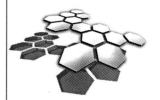

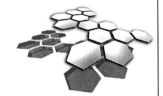

BUILDING EFFECTIVE COMMUNICATION IN THE SMALL GROUP

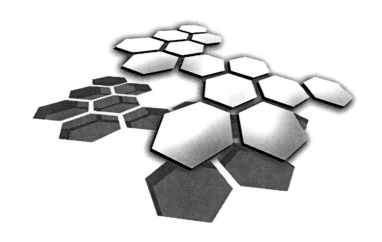

Building Effective Communication in the Small Group
Chapter Thirteen

One of the greatest indicators of a healthy, successful small group is open and free communication. This doesn't happen by accident, but is developed through implementing effective communication principles with the people attending your group. The following section has been taken from *The Ultimate Journey*[1] and adapted for small group training.

Understanding the Social Needs of Your Small Group

One reason people return to your meetings is that they find meaningful friendships with others. Research indicates that if a new person in your church cannot identify seven new friends made in church within the first six months, the chances are very good that they will drop out of active attendance. To view the church as a place where only spiritual needs are to be met is counterproductive to growth. Human beings do have spiritual needs, and where better for these to be met than in church? But people have other needs as well. The church is also a place where emotional, intellectual, and social needs can be met. God puts the solitary in families. If we minister to the whole person, we will reach the multitudes.

A small group is the perfect place to begin addressing and meeting social needs. This is a primary focus of a small group. There are three main social needs to consider:

1. **The Need to be Accepted:** Many come with the desire to be accepted. This need is met as members of the group accept new people on equal terms and begin to develop relationships with them.

2. **The Need to Belong:** Each person has a desire to belong. Belonging involves participation with others. It does not usually come from simply attending and sitting quietly in a meeting. This need goes unmet if a group has no vehicle to bring the new person into active participation.

3. **The Need for Significance:** Self-esteem is built through belonging, while self-worth is built through feeling significant. People want to do something that makes a difference. They want others to need them. They want to feel like their lives are of value to others and to God. We recognize that our self-esteem and self-worth must ultimately come from building our lives on the Rock. There is also, however, a place in God's Kingdom where we are to meet these needs.

Understanding the Process of Communication

There are five distinct levels of communication. Although some relationships can start at deeper levels of conversation, most follow a typical pattern. Knowing these steps will help you in planning your meetings and in assessing the progress of relationships within the groups. These tips will help you, especially in the early stages of forming your group.

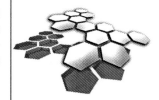

1. **Surface Level Communication:** Most new friendships start with communication about the weather, hobbies, and other "surface level" topics. This level is usually predominant in the first few small group meetings. It serves as a starting point to go to deeper levels of communication during subsequent meetings.

2. **Information Level Communication:** After people have shared with others about non-personal surface topics, they normally shift into sharing factual information about themselves. This usually does not include their feelings or opinions, and rarely includes their beliefs about religion.

3. **Personal Opinion Level Communication:** Once people have reached this point, they are willing to share ideas and opinions about themselves and their beliefs. This begins a deeper level of communication and friendship. This step does not take place until a person feels trust in those around him.

4. **Personal Feeling Level Communication:** This level is only reached when a person feels both trust and friendship with others. During this level people are willing to share what they feel, not just what they think.

5. **Deepest Level Communication:** Intimate friendships and commitments with others are made possible when you have the deepest level communication with a person. Your close friends are those with whom you can share your feelings, your problems, and your innermost struggles. It is with these individuals you have the freedom to be transparent and vulnerable.

Each time you have a meeting, the process of deepening relationships should occur. Recognize this process, and be sensitive in the beginning weeks not to try to force deeper levels of communication. As your group matures, you will want to guide the group into increasing depths of communication.

Effective Verbal Communication Skills

One of the ingredients needed to have a successful small group is good communication skills. Good communication will facilitate healthy relationships. NavPress has a section in their book, *Small-group Training*, which lists effective verbal and non-verbal communication skills. We have included them here for your benefit.

1. **Listening:** Physically and emotionally focus on the person who is talking; showing them your interest and intention to listen. Face the person to whom you are listening; lean forward if you are sitting, relax, and maintain good eye contact. Use brief phrases like "yes, really?" and "how interesting!" to show the person you are attentive. Listening is an art, and is as important to effective communication as speaking.

2. **Seeking Information and Opinions:** Use questions with members who have not spoken recently, and those who have good ideas or opinions. The use of first names is important. Examples are; "Mary, what do you think about the second question?" and "Joe, I'd be interested in your opinion on this subject."

3. **Clarifying:** Misunderstanding can arise when we assume we understand a speaker's meaning. When the meaning is unclear, ask a question for clarification. Examples are: "I'm not sure what you meant. Could you please restate that?" and "Could you repeat that and say a little more

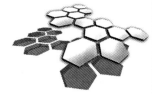

about what you mean?" Clarification is complimentary, because it shows a person you are listening and attentive.

4. **Paraphrasing:** A listener restating a person's thought or idea in his own words demonstrates careful listening and concern. Examples are; "This is what I heard you saying... Is that it?" and "Mark, your central concern is—" or "David, your reactions seem to be—"

5. **Justifying:** This involves asking people to give reasons for what they have said, and should be done in a positive, non-argumentative way. Justifying helps a group stay on the subject. Examples are; "Where do you find that in the passage we're studying?" and "Why do you say that?" and "What is the connection between what we were discussing and your comment?"

6. **Redirecting:** Redirecting should be done if a group member addresses all his questions and comments to the leader rather than to the group. Using names, encourage members to talk with each other. If Mary continues to focus on the leader, the leader might respond to her question, "Tom, what do you think about Mary's last question?" and "How would you answer that, Tom?" This is particularly effective in involving a new member in the discussion.

7. **Extending:** This involves adding to or extending a line of thought in a discussion. After an answer is given or a comment is made, the leader might ask, "Does any one have anything to add to what has been said?" or, "Is there anything else someone would like to comment on at this point?"

8. **Summarizing:** At various points in a group discussion, it is helpful to briefly summarize and highlight what has been previously said. This technique works effectively when a group gets bogged down, since it outlines where the discussion has been and should be going. Mention the group members' names and ideas as you summarize.

9. **Affirming:** It is always important to recognize and affirm the person who is talking. To one you might say, "Thank you for your comment." To another you might add, "That's an interesting point." Never tell a person he is wrong. Simply redirect the question to others by saying; "What do the rest of you think?" The person speaking is important even if a comment seems unimportant.

10. **Being Concrete and Personal:** Use "I" messages instead of "you" messages. Communication improves when members take responsibility for their own ideas and feelings. To say "I feel" and "I think" is much more direct and helpful than "Some people think" or "Some believe."

11. **Being Personally Implicated:** When a discussion seems too general, vague, or abstract, a "personal implication question" helps conversations become more direct and specific. Examples are: "What is your opinion about that?" "How would what you are talking about affect you" and "Sometimes we are abstract when discussing Scripture; how does it affect you day to day?"

12. **Handling Talkative and Silent Members:** Excessively talkative members can be handled through the proper use of group dynamics, non-verbal communication, and strategic seating arrangement. The leader should

break eye contact with the talkative person (sit beside him, not across from him), and maintain consistent eye contact with a silent member (sit opposite him). When the talkative member pauses in the middle of a lengthy speech, the leader should break in and say, "I'd like to hear from someone who has not spoken yet." The leader might direct a question to a silent member. "Jim, what do you think is meant in verse two?" Problems can cause people to talk too much, so try to visit with the talkative person after the meeting. Ask him to observe the next two meetings and determine who is contributing and who is not.

Review these twelve points during the week and try to incorporate them where needed in each meeting. You will be encouraged by seeing each person feel a part of the meeting, as well as by observing the rapid development of new friendships.

Effective Non-Verbal Communication Skills

There is much more to effective communication than verbal presentations. It has been said, "It's not what you say, but how you say it that counts." Ninety percent of what is communicated is not in the words but in the nonverbal connotations. The leader of the small group must recognize nonverbal communication skills and use them to enhance the meeting. Listed below are more suggestions from Nav-Press.

1. **Actions:** Actions are as important as words in communication. The way a person stands or sits, uses his arms and legs, and makes or does not make eye contact can communicate the message and the intent of the speaker. To create a positive image and communicate a positive message, every action should be relaxed, open, responsive, and attentive. Arms should be relaxed, legs crossed toward the listener, eyes and face showing a pleasant expression and keen attention. Any deviation – legs crossed away from the listener, a frown or grimace, a bored or disinterested look – will undermine even the most positive verbal message.

2. **Articulation:** The difference between effective and ineffective communication is often articulation. Proper articulation requires good vocal inflection, a clear and understandable rate of speech, a pleasant voice tone, and crisp enunciation.

3. **Appearance:** Although a speaker can overcome a negative appearance to effectively communicate, an attractive appearance greatly enhances communication. Good posture, whether the speaker is seated or standing, appropriate, neat clothing, and control of distracting mannerisms all combine to provide a positive appearance.

4. **Awareness:** Although the audience may not be aware of them, effective communication can be enhanced or diminished by many factors. When the speaker is as physically close as possible to the listeners, when he or she pays strict attention to the audience, and when he or she responds quickly to questions and shifts in audience mood, communication effectiveness is enhanced.

5. **Atmosphere:** The setting of a small group meeting greatly affects non-verbal communication. The size of the room and furnishings should always be appropriate for the small group. Furniture and decorations should enhance communication, not serve as a distraction or barrier (For example, a large centerpiece on a coffee table could inhibit conversation). All participants

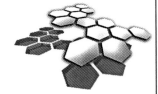

should sit on the same level, not some on chairs and sofas and others on the floor. Room size should be comfortable, neither cramped nor cavernous. When the room is too large for the audience, people should be moved to the front and middle.

Creating Group Discussion Participation

A key ingredient to building relationships is consistent quality interaction. A small group should include discussion, food, and fellowship. These parts of the small group are designed to include every person in the meeting. As you follow the principles outlined, you will see even the shy and timid individuals become involved. The following suggestions can be of further help while planning your group meeting.

1. **Give Every Person Ownership:** Don't monopolize discussion times or group interaction times. Let individuals feel like it is their group. Be patient to allow everyone ample time to respond to questions. Use the word "our" when referring to anything concerning the meeting.

2. **Delegate Leadership Tasks:** Select a different person each time there is a group discussion question. Give each person an opportunity to read Scripture or give an opinion. In addition to providing a sense of ownership, this will also give you an opportunity to find out more about each individual.

3. **Use Open-ended Questions:** Ask questions that require more than a "yes" or "no" response. An example would be: "Dave, what is your opinion of the point Mary just made?", instead of, "Dave, do you agree with what Mary said?" The first question requires a response, but the second question only requires a reply.

4. **Use Visitors for Tasks:** Use visitors to help with the many small tasks needed to be done in the meeting. If you are passing out papers or handbooks, ask a pre-believer to help. They may also assist in setting up the food and fellowship time.

5. **Remain Positive:** Each person must feel the freedom to express his opinions or answer without being intimidated or put down. Don't be negative! Encourage people in their responses even if they are incorrect, and redirect the response to the right answer. An example is: "Mark, thanks so much for that input. Your response does cover part of the answer, but there is still one other part I am looking for. Can anyone add to Mark's thoughts?"

6. **Don't be the Expert:** There will be times people will give incorrect responses. Instead of immediately jumping into giving the correct answer, redirect it to the group. This could be done by saying: "Would anyone else like to respond to the question and give an opinion?"

7. **Set Rules for Discussion Times:** It is helpful to establish a one-minute time limit for each question asked to eliminate one person from controlling the meeting.

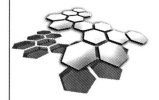

Practical Principles for An Effective Small Group

In Neal F. McBride's book, *How to Lead Small Groups*[2], he lists practical principles for effective small groups. These principles provide useful guidelines to make a small group as successful as possible.

Principle 1: People join groups in order to satisfy some individual need. A person's primary motivation for small group membership is usually self-centered.

Principle 2: A person will remain in (or join) a small group if he finds the group's goals and activities attractive and rewarding. People base their participation on personal standards.

Principle 3: People prefer to participate in groups where other people are similar in age, attractiveness, attitude, personality, economic status, perceived ability, and needs.

Principle 4: Total overall participation in a small group decreases with increasing group size. The larger the group, the less its individual members participate in the discussion, activities, and so on.

Principle 5: Group members usually evaluate smaller groups more positively than larger groups.

Principle 6: The physical setting in which the group meets affects members' attitudes and actions and, consequently, helps determine group process. The meeting place, either positively or negatively, influences members' participation in the group.

Principle 7: Members are more highly motivated and perform more efficiently when the group possesses clear goals and an understanding of what must be done to accomplish the goals. Knowing why the group exists and how it achieves its purposes stimulates higher levels of participation.

Principle 8: Interpersonal relations are generally more positive in situations where goals are mutually derived and accepted. Shared ownership of goals builds positive interaction among the members.

Principle 9: Group performance is facilitated to the extent that people can freely communicate their feelings or satisfaction with the group's progress toward goals. Successful groups talk about and assess their goal achievement.

Principle 10: Groups whose members are heterogeneous with respect to sex and personality types are more conforming and perform more effectively than groups that are homogeneous with respect to these characteristics. The opposite is true for age. Diversity among the members in some areas is helpful to the group's success.

Principle 11: Greater conformity with group norms occurs in groups with decentralized leadership. When the group members share discussion times it promotes compliance with group norms.

[1] Marc Estes, *The Ultimate Journey*: Discussion Groups about Life, City Christian Publishing, copyright 1999

[2] Neal F. McBride, *How to Lead Small Groups*, NavPress, copyright 1990, pp.57-58.

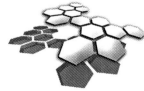

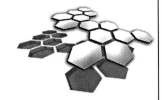

KEY TO FILL-INS

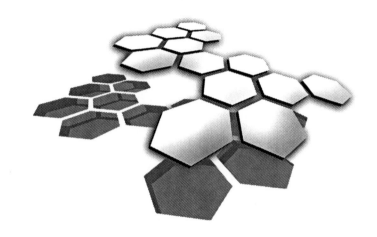

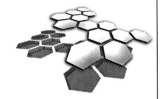

Key to Fill-Ins

Page 16 ..... Clear Vision Provides the Church .... *with clear direction*
Clear Vision Enables the Church .... *to move together*
Clear Vision is the .... *lifeblood of motivation*

Page 21 ..... Importance of Relationship .... *is established in the God-head*
Small Group Concept in the .... *Old Testament*
Small Group Concept in the ministry ... *of Jesus*
Page 22 ..... Small Group Concept in the .... *New Testament Church*

Page 23 ..... 1. *A powerful* .... Church
2. *A witnessing* .... Church
3. *A praying* .... Church
4. *A unified* .... Church
5. *A Spirit-filled* .... Church
6. *A word/teaching* .... Church
7. *A reverent* .... Church
8. *A sharing* .... Church
Page 24 ..... 9. *A gathering-together* .... Church
10. *A supernatural* .... Church
11. *A fellowshipping* .... Church
12. *A rejoicing* .... Church
13. *A worshipping* .... Church
14. *An appealing and relevant* .... Church
15. *A growing and expanding* .... Church

Page 25 ..... Growth Factor #1 .... *The Balanced Heartbeat of the Congregation and Small Groups*

Congregation	Small Group
1. *Celebration*	1. *Infiltration*
2. *Preaching*	2. *Sharing*
3. *Direction*	3. *Discipling*
4. *Equipping*	4. *Encouraging*
5. *Building/Edification*	5. *Expanding/Evangelizing*

Growth Factor #2 .... *The Identifying and Releasing of Lay Leadership*

Page 26 ..... Fourfold Purpose of Small Groups

1. *Relationship*	2. *Pastoral Care*
3. *Equipping*	4. *Evangelism*

Page 37 ..... *A Called* .... Leader
Page 38 ..... *A Spiritual* .... Leader
A Growing .... Leader
A Praying .... Leader
A Godly .... Leader
Page 39 ..... *A Family* .... Leader
A Prudent .... Leader
Page 40 ..... *A Team* .... Leader
Page 41 ..... *A Servant* .... Leader
A Supportive .... Leader

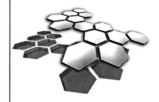

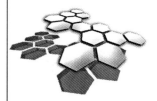

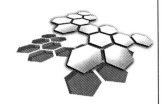

APPENDIX

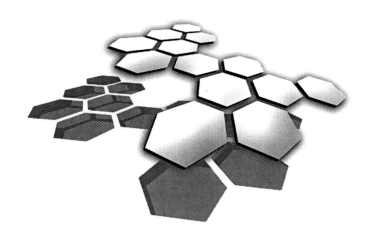

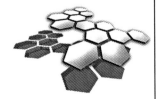

Appendix

The following section contains examples of information and forms that are used at City Bible Church.

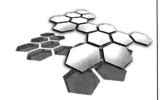

City Bible Church Vision Statement
(Referred to on page 16)

Exalting the Lord... By dynamic, Holy Spirit-inspired worship, praise, prayer, and giving our time, talents, and gifts as an offering to the Lord.

Equipping the Saints... To fulfill their destiny through Godly vision, biblical teaching, and pastoral ministries, bringing believers to maturity in Christ and effective ministry, resulting in a restored triumphant church.

Extending the Kingdom... Of God through the church, to our city, our nation, and the world, through aggressive evangelism, training leaders, planting churches, and sending missionaries and missions teams to our Jerusalem, Judea, Samaria, and the uttermost parts of the earth.

City Bible Church Vision Values
(Referred to on page 17)

The elders and congregation hold in high regard certain biblical values that are the building blocks of our vision. Without these values, the vision would be nothing more than mere words and would result in institutionalism. These values breathe life into the vision and sustain the quality of the vision.

The Value of God's Word
We believe that the Bible is God's inspired Word, the authoritative and trustworthy rule of faith and practice for all Christians.

The Value of God's Manifested Presence
To enjoy God's presence is our passion as a church. We believe there is a presence of God available to God's people as we follow the pattern of worship as seen in the Psalms (see Psalms 22:3).

The Value of Holy Spirit Activity
In both our personal and corporate life as believers, we welcome the moving of the Holy Spirit. The baptism of the Holy Spirit and the gifts of the Holy Spirit are part of our basic belief system and practice.

The Value of the Family
We express this commitment in our strong emphasis on family in preaching, teaching, available counseling, specialized ministries, home school program, and our K-12 Christian school.

The Value of Dynamic, Spontaneous Praise and Worship
Our response to God's presence is seen in our enthusiastic worship: clapping, lifting hands, and singing spontaneous, unrehearsed songs to the Lord.

The Value of Unity
Our goal is not conformity, but unity of spirit and purpose. Unity allows members to express themselves in a variety of ways while still maintaining the same principles and convictions. In this way we flow together in accomplishing vision.

The Value of Holiness

Holiness is not legalism that is measured by outward appearance, but a true cleansing of the believer by the power of the Holy Spirit, evidenced by Christian character and conduct.

The Value of Fervent Prayer

We believe that intercession is the call of every believer. Therefore, the voice of prayer is heard as we pray aloud together in our opening service prayer times. We believe this principle of prayer to be the engine of power in our church life. This is accomplished by individuals praying and fasting, and by a continual and primary emphasis on congregational prayer.

The Value of Reaching the Lost

We believe that every believer is called to reach those individuals who do not have a personal relationship with Jesus Christ. We are committed to remain aggressive in reaching our entire city, state, nation, and world with the message of the Gospel.

The Value of Excellence

We believe God deserves the best we have to offer. Therefore, we seek to maintain a high level of excellence in everything connected to the work of God.

The Value of Relationships

Loving one another is our goal. We work to make this practical through small groups, where every believer is encouraged to develop deeper relationships with other believers.

The Value of Integrity

There is no substitute for godly character. We hold this value in highest esteem and filter all other values through this one. Uprightness, trustworthiness, and transparency are our best foundation stones.

The Value of the Kingdom of God

We desire to positively influence the culture in which we live. We are to be salt and light to the world around us as we penetrate the political, social, and educational arenas with God's Spirit and Word.

Healthy Member Profile
(Referred to on page 26)

The goal of our ministry to every member is to help them to become a person who is born again, water baptized, and filled with the Spirit, who is faithful to the corporate church gathering, Small group ministry and School of Equipping, and actively serving in a place of ministry; joyfully gives their tithe and offerings, enjoys the Word, prayer, and worship, has a heart for winning our city to Christ and a vision of world missions, upholds family values, and loves God with all their heart, soul, mind, and strength.

Healthy Small Group Profile
(Referred to on page 26)

The goal of our Small Group Ministry is to minister to each person who calls City Bible Church their home church. Each Small Group is a network of relationships that assist in creating a smaller family of believers, each devoted one to another. The Small Group is the primary tool used to provide nurture and care to the entire church body. The Small Group is also to be a group of believers excited to share their faith with others, bringing them to Christ. Ultimately, each Small Group should be consistently winning the lost, raising new leaders, and birthing new Small Groups on a regular basis.

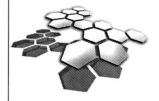

Small Group Structure
(Referred to on page 31)

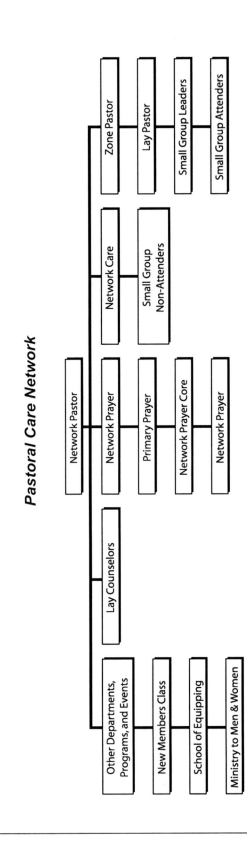

Pastoral Care Network

Defining Ministry Positions
(Referred to on page 32)

The Small Group Network is made up of hundreds of people; all providing their area of gifting and expertise. Every person is important to the overall success of the Small Group Network.

The following section gives a brief description of the different positions and their responsibilities concerning the Small Group Network. Please keep in mind that many of these individuals are involved in other ministries as well.

Elder (see I Peter 5:1-2; I Timothy 5; Titus 1:5; James 5:14)
The form of local church government embraced by City Bible Church is an Elder-ship-ruling church. This form of government is made up of several appointed ministers (spiritual elders) working together in shepherding and guiding the congregation. Together, they operate in a "team ministry" format.

All major directional and visionary decisions concerning small groups are first discussed and approved by the Eldership team before being implemented on the church level.

Senior Pastor (see Acts 14:14, 21-23; 15:6, 22; 20:28-31; 21:17-18)
The Senior Pastor is the "set man." He is the one who guides and directs the overall vision of the church through his discerning of where the Spirit is leading. He is the one who sets both the course and the pace of the entire church, including the Small Group Network. Listed below is a brief ministry description for the Senior Pastor and his relationship to the Small Group Network.

1. The Senior Pastor is responsible for setting the overall vision and direction for all small group decisions.

2. The Senior Pastor meets frequently with the leadership of the small groups to assist in planning and implementing all aspects of the Small Group Network, including all administrative, outreach, and pastoral aspects.

3. The Senior Pastor implants and maintains vision and momentum in the overall church body through various means of communication (i.e. corporate services, leadership training, special events, correspondence, etc).

4. The Senior Pastor is involved in the development of all materials needed for Small Group Leaders: training, notes and updates, growth plans and forecasts, etc.

5. The Senior Pastor is involved in leadership training with all Network Pastors, Lay Pastors, Small Group Leaders, Assistants, and Hosts.

Director of Pastoral Ministries
The Director of Pastoral Ministries has been appointed by the Senior Pastor to oversee all pastoral aspects of the church, which function primarily through the Small Group Network. Listed below is a brief ministry description of the Director of Pastoral Ministries.

1. The Director of Pastoral Ministries meets with the Senior Pastor to discuss all ideas and needs concerning Small Group Network. He is the primary individual to oversee and implement all components of the Pastoral and small group of the local church.

2. The Director of Pastoral Ministries is responsible to maintain the pulse on the pastoral arm of the church and work closely with the Senior Pastor and Pastoral team in making any changes necessary in order to maintain the health and ongoing growth of the church. This may include the development, modification or removal of programs, procedures, policies, etc.

3. The Director of Pastoral Ministries meets regularly with all Network Pastors for accountability and assistance in the needs or concerns of each Network.

4. The Director of Pastoral Ministries oversees all administrative tasks, including but not limited to the following: data management, monthly reporting, development of materials, leadership training, managing the small group center, and correspondence with all Network Pastors, Lay Pastors, and Small Group Leaders.

Network Pastors

The Small Group Network is divided into twelve specific districts. There are six geographic networks and five specialized networks: Ethnic Cells, New Life Cells, Youth Cells, Impact Singles Cells, and Portland Bible College Cells. Although each Network may vary due to the special needs and demographics of a particular region, the responsibilities are the same. Listed below is a brief ministry description of the Network Pastors and their relationship to the Small Group Network.

1. The husband-wife team functions together in all areas of pastoral ministry. They follow the Priscilla/Aquilla model of being pastoral ministers, with a love of people, the gift of hospitality and skill in equipping leaders.

2. The Network Pastor is a mission-minded leader, with a five-fold level of gifts, and abilities to counsel, teach, train, equip, and administer a large group of people (see Ephesians 4:11-12).

3. The spouse complements the team with specific strengths. The spouse should have an above-average gift in hospitality, the ability to assist in administrative needs in the district, the ability to counsel in the district, and should assist in pastoral ministry.

4. The Network Pastor assists in recruiting, developing, training, and encouraging Zone Pastors, Lay Pastors, Small Group Leaders, and Assistants.

5. The Network Pastor recruits new leaders and creates new groups within their network based upon the growth of their particular network.

6. The Network Pastor assists in maintaining ongoing training for any new or existing leaders within their network.

7. The Network Pastor will work closely with all Zone Pastors and Lay Pastors to ensure all people within their network are receiving proper pastoral care.

8. The Network Pastor will work closely with the Assimilation Department in making sure all new people attending the church are assimilated into the small group ministry.

9. The Network Pastor will work closely with the Evangelism Department and

assist in all outreaches either church-wide or in their network.

10. The Network Pastor will meet frequently with all network leaders for prayer and spiritual input, and for discussion of the health of the network and any long-range plans.

Zone Pastors

As each network grows in numbers, the need for additional senior network leadership is essential to properly lead the Lay Pastors. Once a network has exceeded fifteen small groups, a Zone Pastor should be appointed to assist the Network Pastor in their responsibilities. Just as with other tiers of leadership, there is no limit to the number of Zone Pastors a Network might have.

A Zone Pastor is simply one who has the pastoral/equipper gift, who is trained and released to do the work of pastoring, but who is not necessarily ordained as an elder. Listed below is a brief ministry description of the Zone Pastors and their relationship to the Small Group Network.

1. The Zone Pastor works with the Network Pastor in overseeing the growth strategy, development of ministries, raising leaders and pastoral needs of a network.

2. The Zone Pastor oversees a defined group or an entire region of the city (a zip code, or multiple zip codes depending on the concentration of people) and takes care of any needs that arise in that particular region.

3. The Zone Pastor will assist the Network Pastor in maintaining all prayer ministry in the network, working closely with the Network Prayer Coordinator, the Network Core and the Prayer Network.

4. The Zone Pastor oversees several Lay Pastors and works closely with each leader to provide resources, encouragement and ongoing training to keep every small group healthy and filled with healthy members.

5. The Zone Pastor provides Lay Pastors with regular evaluations of the network progress.

6. The Zone Pastor ensures that Lay Pastors work to mobilize network leadership into regular birthing of small groups, and that new leadership is being enlisted into areas of active service.

7. The Zone Pastor engages in crisis counseling on most of the severe problems encountered in their area of oversight. The Zone Pastor will ask for assistance from the Network Pastor and transfer moral cases and matters involving child abuse, homosexuality, divorce, divorce/remarriage, and offenses causing someone to leave the church. They will provide the Lay Pastors and Small Group Leaders with training and support in all less serious counseling needs.

8. The Zone Pastor commits to three to five years of service.

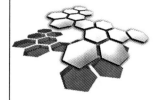

Lay Pastors

One of the most important links in the Small Group Network is the position of the Lay Pastor. This group of very qualified and gifted leaders have become the pastoral/equipping force in the church. A Lay Pastor is simply one who has the pastoral/equipper gift, who is trained and released to do the work of pastoring and raising leaders, but who is not necessarily ordained as an elder. Listed below is a brief ministry description of the Lay Pastors and their relationship to the Small Group Network.

1. The Lay Pastor works with the Network Pastor in overseeing the pastoral needs of a network.

2. The Lay Pastor oversees a defined group or an entire region of the city (a zip code, or multiple zip codes depending on concentration of people) and takes care of any needs that arise in that particular region.

3. The Lay Pastor oversees several small groups and works closely with each leader to provide information, facilitate, communicate, problem-solve, encourage, train, and pastor.

4. The Lay Pastor meets regularly with their Small Group Leaders to discuss the goals of developing healthy members and healthy small groups with the use of the Analysis Chart and the Personal Growth Chart.

5. The Lay Pastor ensures that Small Group Leaders mobilize their members into areas of active service and ministry, resulting in each member potentially becoming involved in some form of small group leadership themselves. This would include regular small group birthing in each individual group.

6. The Lay Pastor works closely with the Assimilation department in connecting new people to the small group that best fits their particular need.

7. The Lay Pastor engages in pastoral ministry counseling on most of the problems encountered in the small groups they oversee. Most common-care counseling remains with the Small Group Leader. Issues such as general marriage and financial counseling will remain with the Lay Pastor. The more serious cases, such as moral cases, child abuse, homosexuality, divorce, divorce/remarriage, and offenses causing someone to leave the church will be deferred to the Zone Pastor or Network Pastor.

8. The Lay Pastor commits to three to five years of service.

Small Group Coaches

The Small Group Coach represents more of a function than an actual position. A Small Group Coach is someone who assists a newly appointed Small Group Leader in establishing their small group over a twelve-week period using the Small Group Leader Coaching Guide.

All levels of district leadership (Network Pastor, Zone Pastor, Lay Pastor, and Small Group Leader) may be a Small Group Coach. This allows the opportunity for maximum growth in each network without 'bottlenecking' any particular tier of leadership.

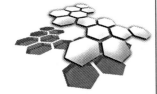

Small Group Leaders

The Small Group Leader is the key to successfully pastoring and growing the church. Each leader is involved in frequent contact with the people who attend the group. It is this group of leaders that are instrumental in shepherding, discipling the church, and equipping each member to reach our city for Christ.

A detailed description of the duties and responsibilities can be found in the handbook. Below is a very brief outline of the tasks of a Small Group Leader.

1. The Small Group Leader oversees a designated group of people and acts as a facilitator of the church vision.

2. The Small Group Leader works with the leadership of the church in guiding, discipling, training, mobilizing, releasing, and shepherding a particular group of people.

3. The Small Group Leader assists in mobilizing their group to reach unbelievers with the gospel.

4. The Small Group Leader works to create a sense of community among the people within their group.

5. The Small Group Leader is involved in common-care counseling.

6. The Small Group Leader makes a two-year commitment.

7. The Small Group Leader serves twelve to twenty people.

8. The Small Group Leader regularly births new small groups to ensure ongoing growth and a balanced span of pastoral care for all individuals.

Assistant Small Group Leaders

Assistants are involved in a small group for two main reasons. First, they are to assist the Small Group Leader in all aspects of their group. Second, they are being trained to become a Small Group Leader. Each small group may have more than one Assistant. Listed below is a brief description of the Assistant Small Group Leader's ministry.

1. The Assistant Small Group Leader assists the Small Group Leader in the ongoing duties of running a successful, healthy group which embraces the church vision.

2. The Assistant Small Group Leader works with the leadership of the church in guiding, discipling, training, mobilizing, releasing, and shepherding a particular group of people.

3. The Assistant Small Group Leader assists in mobilizing their group to reach unbelievers with the gospel.

4. The Assistant Small Group Leader helps the Leader in any common-care counseling.

5. The Assistant Small Group Leader makes a two-year commitment.

6. The Assistant Small Group Leader receives any training necessary in order to become a Small Group Leader.

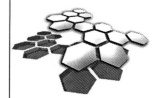

7. The Assistant Small Group Leader is ready to take their own small group within one year of becoming an Assistant and will assist in training a new Assistant.

8. The Assistant Small Group Leader assists in serving from twelve to twenty people.

Host Home

The environment in which a small group meets can determine the overall success of the group. A host home is an intricate part of the Small Group Network. Each group may have more than one Host. Listed below is a brief description of the host.

1. The Host has the gift of hospitality demonstrated by the desire to open their home to become a ministry center for the church.

2. The Host Home provides a comfortable atmosphere for the small group meeting.

3. The Host works closely with the Small Group Leader in setting specific house rules for behavior in the home.

4. The Host assists the Small Group Leader with any specific needs concerning the group.

Potential Leaders

In order for every small group to fulfill its purpose of meeting needs, reaching the lost, raising leaders and birthing new groups, there must be a continual effort to identify future leaders. The Potential Leader position has been created to offer young leaders a chance to get further involved in small group ministry without feeling overwhelmed with the position or function of a Leader or Assistant. This also allows each Leader to groom young leaders and mentor them into future levels of leadership without having the pressures associated with young, inexperienced leaders.

Requirements and Qualifications of a Small Group Leader
(Referred to on page 49)

Listed below are the requirements and qualifications necessary to become a Small Group Leader at City Bible Church.

1. Must be an official member of our church.

2. Attend weekend services regularly, including School of Equipping.

3. Faithful tither.

4. Complete the Small Group Leaders Training Course.

5. Begin the small group birthing process with a Small Group Coach and by using the Small Group Leaders Coaching Guide.

6. Should be functioning according to 1 Timothy 5 and Titus 1.

7. Able to make a two-year commitment to leading a Small Group.

8. Capable and committed to leading their flock into ongoing community as well as conducting regular small group meetings.

9. Able to lead a small group meeting following approved materials, to communicate well, and to lead discussions.

10. Able to facilitate meetings: keep order, stay focused, follow up needs, phone and visit group members, and minister to the pastoral needs of the group.

11. Have a vision for evangelism and the ability to equip and inspire the entire group to reach their neighbors and bring them into a healthy relationship with Christ, His church, and His cause.

12. Work closely with the Evangelism Department and Lay Pastors, helping assimilate new people into their small group.

13. Meet with their Lay Pastor in scheduled monthly meetings, keeping them informed of all critical needs in the group, and meet monthly with the Network leadership team.

14. Faithfully attend the Network Summit meeting with the Senior Pastor.

Personal Growth & Development Chart

District #_____

District Pastor

Lay Pastor

Small Group Leader

Name

Stage	Category	Role	Item
Infancy	CALLING	Member - M	Salvation / Turning Points
			Water Baptized
			Holy Spirit Baptized
			Attends Weekend services regularly
			Attends Small Groups regularly
			Attends School of Equipping
			Gives Tithes and Offerings
			Enjoys regular personal prayer, Word, and worship
			Heart for winning the lost / City & World
			Upholds family values
			Completed New Members class
			Loves God with heart, soul, mind, and strength
Childhood	TRAINING	Potential Leader - PL	NP/LP approval for Potential Leader
			Good People skills
			Servant attitude
			Emotionally stable
			Strong character
			Performs tasks effectively
			Follows through
			Makes right decisions
			Family / marriage in order
Adolescence	SENDING	Assistant Leader - A	NP/LP approval for Assistant
			Complete Small Group Leader's Training
			Train/Assist discussion times
			Train/Assist planning meeting
			Train/Assist pastoral care
			Train/Assist outreach
			Train/Assist assimilation
			Train/Assist counseling
			Train/Assist administration/reports/forms
			Train/Assist running entire group
			Earned respect and trust of people
Marriage	REPRODUCING	Cell Leader - L	NP/LP approval for new Small Group birth
			Plan type and timing of Group
			Choose team
			Contact Small Group Leader
			Plan date to launch new Group
			Plan Cell "Send Out" meeting
			Contact LP/DP to Attend
			Send out new Small Group team
			Contact frequently

Small Group Options
(Referred to on page 33)

Regional Groups
These groups form based on geography. They may include people who live in a particular neighborhood, ZIP code, or school district. Individuals who have relationships with those in the group but who do not themselves live in the given geographical area may be part of the group as well.

Service Groups
Designed to utilize the gifts, talents, skills, and abilities of group members, the focus of these groups is meeting the needs of others.

- Food and Clothing Ministry
- Big Brother / Big Sister
- After-school tutors
- Crisis support (birth, illness, death)
- Never Alone (for shut-ins)
- Helping Hands (repairs)
- Hospitality team

Recreation Groups
These groups bring together those who share similar recreational interests.

- Soccer / Softball
- Fishing / Hunting
- Bicycling / Mountain Biking
- Rock Climbing
- PSU Football / Rockies Baseball
- Games (CashFlow, Settlers of Katan)
- Snowboarding / Skateboarding
- Walking / Hiking
- Golfing
- Running / Jogging
- Workout / Aerobics

Special Interest Groups
These groups gather together those who have special interests or hobbies

- Computer Club
- Scrapbooking
- SuperShoppers
- MOPS (Mothers of Preschoolers)
- Investment Club
- Older Singles
- Quilting
- Crafts / Arts
- Birdwatching
- Tea & Tots playgroups
- Cooking / Baking

Life-skills Groups
Geared to assist those who desire further coaching in specific areas using God's word and life experiences of others.

- Men's/Women's Bible Studies
- ALPHA course
- Blended Family Group
- Moms with a Mission
- Finance / Budgeting
- Weight Maintenance

Support Groups
Assisting those looking for extra care, support and counseling in areas of struggle.

- Celebrate Recovery
- Divorce Recovery
- Men of Purpose (pornography recovery)
- Prodigal Loved Ones
- Grief Support
- Victory over Addictions

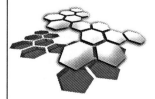

City Bible Church
Pastoral Care Flow Chart

SOURCES ■
CLASSIFIERS ●
FULFILLERS □

HEALTHY, ACTIVE REPRODUCING MEMBER OF CBC

CITY REACH ASSIMILATION DEPARTMENT
Food/Clothing

DELIVERANCE MINISTRY
Pastoral Counseling
One-Time Encounter
All Things New Weekend

NETWORK LAY COUNSELOR
Specialized Issues
Long-Term Needs

SMALL GROUP LEADER
Common Care
Basic Instruction
General Counseling
Food & Clothing
Helps

NETWORK LAY PASTOR
Crisis Counseling
Pre-Marital Counseling
Marital Conflict
Financial Counseling
Offenses

NETWORK LAY PASTOR
Sever Marital Problems
Members Leaving Church
Sexual Sins/Legal Issues
Abuse & Addiction
Severe Marital Crisis

NON CBC ATTENDER

CBC ATTENDER NON SMALL GROUP ATTENDER

CBC ATTENDER SMALL GROUP ATTENDER

NETWORK MINISTRIES COORDINATOR
Determines Need

ASSIMILATION DEPARTMENT

WEEKEND SERVICE
Incoming Need
Counseling
Information Card
Next Step Form
Altar

CHURCH OFFICE
Walk-in/Call-in
Other Departments
Incoming Need
Counseling

CITY CARE
Incoming
Pastoral Need

NETWORK CARE
Incoming
Pastoral Need